RESTORING THE YEARS THE LOCUSTS HAVE EATEN

Endorsements

"This book is a powerhouse, full stop. Its authority feels undeniable. Leah's story is such a testimony and demands to be heard."

Erich Hofmeister

"Important & Powerful"

Ann Kafer

"Insightful, inspirational & invigorating"

Tess Kossow

In this vivid book, *Restoring the Years the Locusts Have Eaten*, Leah shares her journey within an emotionally abusive marriage and how she wrestled with divorce as a Christian woman. Leah uses her powerful story along with Scripture to demonstrate and reinforce God's deep love and ability to restore our lives. Readers will find inspiration, challenges, and practical tools to escape the spiritual bondage of chronic abuse. Her book offers crucial support, empowering women to make informed decisions about staying in or leaving such relationships. The book is also an essential resource for pastors, counselors, friends, and family members walking through these issues with women they love.

RESTORING THE YEARS THE LOCUSTS HAVE EATEN

Rescued for a Purpose:
Emotional Freedom After Abuse

Leah Hoppes

Restoring the Years the Locusts Have Eaten

Copyright © 2024 by Leah Hoppes.

All Rights Reserved.

Requests for information should be addressed to:
Vision Force Media, C/O
Vision Force, LLC, 473 Dunham Road, Suite 219, St. Charles, IL 60174.

This edition: ISBN: 978-0-9983146-5-5 (paperback)

Library of Congress Control Number: 2024910789

All rights reserved. No part of this book may be used or reproduced, stored in a retrieval system, or transmitted in any form or by any means—electronic, mechanical, photocopy, recording, or other—except for brief quotation in printed reviews without the publisher's prior permission.

This book is based on the narrator's personal experiences, perspectives, and memories. To protect privacy and confidentiality, names, identifying details and certain events have been changed, altered or combined. Any resemblance to real people, living or deceased, is purely coincidental. Neither the publisher nor the author is engaged in providing professional advice or services to the individual reader. The ideas, thoughts, and suggestions in this book are not intended to replace consultation with a qualified mental health professional. It is intended for informational and narrative purposes only and should not be construed as professional advice. Neither the author nor the publisher shall be liable for any loss or damage allegedly arising from any information or suggestions contained in this book. Readers should consult qualified professionals regarding any specific concerns or decisions.

Cover photo: AI Artistry

Interior design: Melissa Castillo

Author photograph: C + M Photography

First printing July 2024: Printed in the United States of America

Dedicated to Marjorie Stradinger

a woman of unwavering faith

"I will restore to you the years which the swarming locust has eaten, the hopper, the destroyer, and the cutter, my great army, which I sent among you." (Joel 2:25 ESV)

TABLE OF CONTENTS

Foreword: Erich Hofmeister xiii

Introduction xvi

SECTION I: THE STORY 1

Chapter 1: The Shot 2

Chapter 2: The Hospital 5

Chapter 3: The Necklace 19

Chapter 4: The Darkness 22

Chapter 5: The Meetings 31

Chapter 6: The Look 38

Chapter 7: The Decision 40

Chapter 8: The Out 46

Chapter 9: The Escape 48

SECTION II: HEALING & RESTORATION 51

Chapter 10: Defiant Hope 52

Chapter 11: Stop the Cycle 62

Chapter 12: Religiosity Problem 69

Chapter 13: Grieve and Grow 97

Chapter 14: Chase Jesus 103

Chapter 15: Accident Waiting 115
Chapter 16: Guide to Healing 120
Chapter 17: Psychological Violence 135

Afterword 146
Resources 149
Acknowledgments 151
About the Author 154

FOREWORD

Let's say you've decided you want to, or even must, climb Mount Everest. Daunting. Intimidating. Almost inconceivably difficult. But yet, there it is – the mountain that lies before you. Immovable, but yet demanding to be scaled. To do so holds the promise of a vista you've never encountered and a freedom and confidence you could perhaps only dream of.

You likely would take this climb very, very seriously. You would have to. This is your life we're talking about. And several people die yearly trying to take it on.

It would be fair to say you would prepare in several ways. Your fitness, mental fortitude, and careful study of the mountain's variables and conditions are all in play.

You also might find it necessary, even essential, to find a guide – someone who knows a thing or two about this very worthy and arguably terrifying opponent. You could seek out someone who has read a lot about the mountain - someone who has researched what it is like to climb and reach the summit. You could find someone who has watched many videos about the behemoth and used all their cognitive faculties to the best of their ability to instruct you on what it *might* be like to face this goliath.

Or you could, instead, hire someone who has climbed Everest.

They might be called mountaineers, Sherpas, or Everest guides, but they must have done the climb and lived to tell about it.

They need to know what it feels like to be ill-equipped, scared, isolated, intimidated, alone, and outmatched. They need to know what it's like to push through the "death zone," disorientation, exhaustion, and how to overcome all the waves of self-doubt and discouragement - then finally, to reach the peak and discover what they might have thought impossible to achieve: Victory. Hope. Freedom - A deep part of themselves restored because of what they courageously faced and moved through.

You haven't chosen this book to learn more about mountains per se. You have likely purchased this book because you are facing or aiming to help others face an incredible challenge. That's what this Everest is - not a person you must defeat, but perhaps a cycle of abuse to end, a destructive relationship to exit, or a grueling divorce to heal from.

You might be seeking answers and insight. Or you may be looking for hope in an often neglected and ignored area. A guide here is invaluable. And to find a guide like the one I described would be to find someone who has *lived* the subject matter at hand.

This is where we find our author, Leah Hoppes.

While Leah's careful and painstaking research for this book is obvious, it is her first-hand encounter with the fires of abuse in her own life that makes her voice clear, potent, and vitally important in our current milieu, both inside and outside of the Church.

I first met Leah while looking for a Marketing Coach for my fledgling business. She stood out immediately. Beyond her expertise and intelligence, she seemed to understand people, and the latter carries vastly more weight than any other attribute.

She brings that to her writing, and it is obvious in these pages. To understand people is to be able to meet them where they are and minister to their needs—and how much more so with a subject matter she knows personally and passionately cares about.

To be a healer is to know the Healer Himself. Those who have been wounded can lead others to healing because of the restoration they've experienced. This is Leah. She knows deeply, and she cares deeply. She is a woman of bold faith, and her message is urgent.

Her intent is plain—she wants us and the Church to apply these hard-won principles so healing and restoration can become more commonplace and produce more hope-filled testimonies.

A short note about me: Before I began working with people as a Transformational Life Coach, I spent the better part of two decades in ministry. I held pastoral roles working with youth and young adults and then went on to co-pastor a congregation while continuously engaged in pastoral and premarital counseling.

While I have some experience coaching and counseling women who have been in abusive situations, it was rare the topics were discussed in depth, both in seminary and in the church where I labored with other pastors. I consider this book the manual I never had but always needed.

The pages that follow not only exhibit a compassionate and serious treatment of the subject matter but also move us into concrete application. This, I believe, equals healing. Leah's story is compelling not only because of the almost unimaginable and harrowing trials she faced but even more because of what she employed by the power of God to overcome and find the restoration she now offers to you, the reader.

May you be blessed to find the freedom and healing that God longs for you to have when you read and apply this book, not only for yourself but for all those you are to affect.

Erich Hofmeister

INTRODUCTION

The biggest challenge in writing this book was addressing the church's response to divorce in situations of abuse. I have witnessed what appears to be false teaching in the church, and I wanted to challenge our approach, specifically in these situations, to better love and serve those living in this turmoil. There are women (and men) who love Jesus but find themselves trapped in a cycle of abuse – forbidden from speaking the truth and forced to lie to protect their family's social façade.

It was critical to bring you into part of my story, not to air dirty laundry but to share enough so that you can relate to or learn from it. I have tried not to offer excuses but simply my perspective so you learn how and why one can stay in such a dishonest and dishonoring marriage for so long.

I invite you to join me in discovering truth, healing, and restoration.

SECTION I
THE STORY

CHAPTER 1
THE SHOT

It was a gorgeous, sunny September day. Joe and I were supposed to attend an event at the gun club near our vacation home. I had recently started enjoying trap shooting, and I was excited that this would be my first chance to try skeet shooting. Since this was a big event, I was also looking forward to meeting other women who shared an interest in shooting.

After getting ready, I reminded Joe that it was time to leave. He changed his mind, as he typically did at the last minute, exchanging time with me, his wife, for solitude – and beer. I tried to convince him to go with me, but he did what he wanted on his terms with no consideration for me. This was typical. Shrugging off the awful feeling of showing up to yet another event without him and excusing his absence always left me feeling icky, but after more than a decade, I had gotten used to it. I would suck it up, cover for him and pretend I was perfectly fine even though I was embarrassed and disappointed.

Once I got to the event, I lined up to try skeet with my shotgun, and the loneliness dissipated as I chatted with others. The excitement of a new skill and hitting my targets let me forget I was there alone.

Skeet shooting uses clay targets, known as "pigeons," which are shot out of a "high house" and a "low house," meaning one can hit two targets instead of one target used in trap shooting. It was fast-paced, which I loved.

Before I continue, here's a brief tutorial on the language used in the sport. Shotguns of varying calibers are used for trap, skeet, and sporting clays. The ammunition used with a shotgun is called a slug or buckshot. When fired, the slug, or shell, is filled with small pellets that dissipate in a spray pattern. When those pellets hit the target, the clay shatters into shards across the sky, a highly satisfying sight. Gunpowder and hunter safety orange clay bits – daytime fireworks!

Some shotguns have two barrels, referred to as "Over-Under" or "Side-by-Side," describing how the barrels are situated in relation to each other. The first means the barrels are attached vertically, and the second means they are beside each other. One more notable distinction: some have two separate triggers, and some have a single trigger. However, even a single trigger does not allow both barrels to be shot simultaneously. Squeeze the trigger once, and the first barrel will fire; squeeze it a second time, and the second barrel will fire. The gun I was using was a .28 caliber over-under with a single trigger. Compared to a .12-gauge shotgun, a .28 gauge is smaller, lighter, and has less recoil.

It was my turn, and I got into position. I yelled, "Pull!" The targets soared into the air.

[*Lead the target. "Bang" *Lead the target "Bang"]

I was hooked! This was more fun than shooting trap! I got up to my turn again and got into position. "Pull!"

[*Lead the first target. "BOOM!"]

It was excruciatingly loud even with my ear protection in. I felt the reverberation through my entire body. The force of the recoil knocked me off balance and spun me to my right. Everyone in line behind me looked as surprised as I felt. "Did both barrels just go off?" a man asked. I replied, "Yes, I think so." This should not have happened, and everyone knew it. We discussed how weird it was. Another member gave me his shotgun on my next turn. As much fun as I was having with what I had determined was my new hobby, my head started to hurt.

Without my other half, my day wasn't as fun as anticipated, so I went into the clubhouse for a soda, hoping a caffeine hit would curb my growing headache. I stayed for another hour, but my headache didn't disappear, so I went home. By the way, despite the misfire, I still hit both targets.

My shoulder and upper arm were severely bruised from the impact of the gun misfire. I had absorbed the recoil of not just a single shot but of both of those barrels firing simultaneously. I didn't feel quite like myself for the next two weeks, but I brushed it off as being tired, having a lot of work, and getting ready for my mom to visit. The events at the gun club were all but forgotten.

CHAPTER 2
THE HOSPITAL

OCTOBER 1

I didn't feel well when I got ready for work that Thursday morning. I couldn't pinpoint what was wrong; I wasn't feverish or nauseous, but I didn't feel "right." I drove to work thinking I'd be fine. A headache started once I was at my desk, and I felt worse. An intense pain developed above my right eye and on the right side of my neck. Coworkers noticed I was pale and not my usual chipper self. They asked me if I was OK, and I responded, "I feel weird." Dave suggested that Lizz drive me home in my car, and he could follow us so he could bring her back to work after they dropped me off. In my typical "I can handle it" attitude at the time, I snipped, "I'm fine." But, after a few more minutes, I thought he was right; perhaps I should go home.

I closed my laptop and placed it in my laptop bag, and when I leaned over to pick it up, my hand didn't want to tighten around the handle. I now knew this was more serious than I initially thought. This was not normal. I took Dave and Lizz up on their offer to drive me home.

As Lizz drove, the pain increased, and I found that applying pressure to my forehead helped. I also noticed that my right arm and the right side of my face felt numb. Lizz asked me a question. My answer was slurred. A warning bell, I never slurred my speech. Friends had always teased me about my articulation; sloppy speech was not normal for me.

I repeated myself, slowly being sure to articulate and still slurred. "This can't be good," I thought to myself. I flipped down the passenger visor and opened the mirror to see if my face was drooping. My face wasn't sagging, but my upper lip was slightly pulled up. I knew something wasn't right. I told Lizz, "I think I'm having a stroke. Take me to the Urgent Care; it's on the way." When we arrived at the Urgent Care parking lot, I opened the car door, exited, and stepped forward, but instead, my body went to the right. I tried again, concentrating on moving forward, but when I took a step, my legs carried me to the right. By now, Dave had parked and rushed to me in order to usher me inside.

Within minutes, I was on an exam table with a doctor asking me questions. Yes, I knew what day it was. Yes, I knew who the President was, and when the doctor made a quasi-political statement, leave it to me to comment on *that*. (*Urgh, why do I do that!?) I stopped myself from saying anything further, recognizing that my life may be in this person's hands.

Moments later, I was rushed into an ambulance and off to the hospital. I couldn't swallow. I felt like I was going to choke. I told the medic that I couldn't swallow my saliva. He told me to turn my head to the side and let it drain out; there was nothing to be embarrassed about. He assured me I would be OK. I was oddly calm for not being able to swallow.

At the ER, I was put through several tests, and my ability to swallow returned. When the test results came back, I overheard a young doctor exclaim, "I was right! It was a VAD!" I remember smiling at his little victory, even though I didn't know what that meant.

Turns out, VAD is a Vertebral Artery Dissection. It's when a piece of the artery lining breaks off from the artery wall. They admitted me to the hospital for an overnight stay.

The next day, my friends from work and even my boss visited and told me I had scared them. I was in good spirits; I laughed, joked, and waited to be released. By Saturday, I learned they wouldn't do the MRI until Sunday, so I likely wouldn't be released until Sunday night or Monday morning.

Two doctors stopped by my room and asked if I had been in a car wreck or maybe had been on a roller coaster recently to determine what caused the VAD. I mentioned the skeet shooting incident the week before and told them I hadn't felt right since then. The two of them exchanged a look and then, just as quickly, said, "No, that wasn't it." My intuition told me they didn't know what I was talking about, but neither would admit it. I decided to let it go.

On Sunday, the MRI confirmed I had not one but two strokes. The neurologist spent a lot of time with me and seemed to enjoy the medical anomaly I presented. Ultimately, he couldn't find a cause for the VAD and ensuing strokes but told me how lucky I was and not to worry; it would never happen again.

I rested easy that night and anticipated being able to go home the next morning.

OCTOBER 5

"Pull the string. I need to pull the string."

A singular thought.

I saw nothing except that emergency pull string installed in hospital bathrooms for help.

As if I were a ghost, I had no sense of my body or extremities. I felt like a floating entity. I couldn't see the tip of my nose or any other body part. I didn't see the railing, the bathroom walls, or the floor. I experienced a sort of tunnel vision with no peripheral vision.

I saw one thing—the string.

I didn't have ten different ideas of 'what if' bouncing around like my typical pinball machine of thoughts. This realm had no inner dialogue, competing thoughts, or anxiousness. I had one singular thought:

"Pull the string."

**

I was being wheeled down a hallway on a hospital bed and felt the uncomfortable bump as we passed the threshold into a room where I saw a nurse's face in mine - smiling. I think she was talking.

**

Perhaps it was the same nurse whose face was right up next to mine, saying they were preparing to put a scope down my throat to see if the strokes were coming from my heart. I had one thought, "Uh oh. When they did that to Dad, he had to learn how to swallow again."

**

I was in a hospital bed, and my eyes were open. I saw my next-door neighbor looking worried and Joe beside her, grinning like a Cheshire cat.

**

I was outside on a gurney. I heard voices discussing a helicopter ride.

**

It was a vivid blue October sky, untarnished by clouds.

[Ratchety, bump. Ratchety, bump. Ratchety, bump. Rachety, bump].

"With all the technology in the world, they can't make smoother gurneys?" It was my only thought—no concern about my situation, no fear – just an instinctual reaction to my discomfort.

**

The hospital sent me from their Level 1 Trauma Center via Life Flight to a university-run Level 1 Trauma Center, hoping they would know how to treat me. I didn't comprehend this during my short bouts of consciousness; this was all filled in for me after the fact.

October 5th was a lost day. No, I didn't hear anything when I was unconscious – no dreams, no visions. Every memory was as if it were immediately following except minutes and hours passed between these moments of awareness.

The medic monitoring me on the helicopter removed the cloth from my eyes, and I squinted as the sunlight was blinding coming through the window. I saw his face briefly as he appeared to be checking on me. The cloth went back over my eyes.

**

I felt jarred as they removed me from the helicopter upon landing; I was aware of a team rushing around me as they wheeled me inside.

**

Multiple sets of hands lifted and laid me on what felt like a cloud. Unlike the previous hospital bed and the 'ratchety, bump' gurney experience, I was gently lifted onto the most luxurious bed I had ever felt, and the pillow hugged my head. What an impossibly divine feeling. I closed my eyes again.

**

I was being prepped for an MRI.

**

It was dark out. I was starving. I asked for something to eat.

**

I was in my new room. Neuro ICU. I asked for something to eat. A young nurse or aide exclaimed, "Wow, she's worse than I thought. She keeps repeating the same thing over and over!" The other nurse laughed gently, "It's the medication; that's what's causing her to do that." It's funny how my brain picked up on that exchange. It was the first memory of more than an in-and-out consciousness I had on that first day. It was the first time my brain could process information beyond an inch from my face. I was finally starting to see and hear about a foot beyond myself. I went from not talking or responding all day to asking for food and hearing the nurses talk about me. It was progress.

RESTORING THE YEARS THE LOCUSTS HAVE EATEN

**

I asked for food again, but I was told they couldn't give me anything until they tested my ability to swallow. I asked for water, but they only brought a cup of ice.

OCTOBER 6

By the next morning, I had regained complete consciousness. I hadn't been expected to make it through the night. I wouldn't find that detail out until much later, either.

My sight was no longer restricted, and I had regained my normal range of vision. The neurologists and neurosurgeons paraded around with their interns. Like a monkey, I obediently touched the pen, touched my nose, and wiggled my toes. My head was pounding, but I was aware of my room and everyone coming in and out.

A bit later, a doctor asked if I knew my name and where I was. I responded correctly. She said, "Do you know why you're here?" Conditioned for years to downplay everything, I replied, "Yes, I had a stroke." Her eyebrows lifted, her pen paused, and she replied, "You had one stroke?" I quickly realized that not giving her an accurate account of my information could be bad for me. She needed to know what information I had. I corrected my reply with, "I had three strokes." She nodded, satisfied with my proper recollection of why I was in the hospital.

Someone had held me to the truth for the first time in my 38 years.

This was new. There was a stirring in my spirit. I had just been allowed to speak to the truth of a situation without judgment and without being repudiated. I shouldn't have been comforted by this, but I was.

She didn't dispute the severity of what had happened. She didn't make it about herself. She didn't tell me it was nothing or that I would be OK — quite the contrary. I was being tested on my cognitive ability so that the medical team could determine any deficiencies from the strokes. I had to hold to the truth of the situation, so she knew I was OK. In the hospital, I couldn't ignore, deny, or otherwise dismiss what had happened. She wouldn't let me.

There was and is so much power in truth.

All the doctors and nurses were kind and attentive. I'd never been so doted on, listened to, or cared for – this felt nice. I was weak but could make a few phone calls to explain what happened. I was not worried or anxious. I felt well taken care of and grateful for the benevolence of the nursing staff. I was strangely happy despite the circumstances.

I slept a lot.

The physical therapist arrived to get me out of bed and walk around the ICU wing. The hospital staff told me how well I was doing and appeared relieved at how well I had recovered.

OCTOBER 7

My mind was quiet. I experienced singular thoughts as my mind responded to the stimuli around me.

The neurosurgeon assigned to me was the one who finally determined the cause of the strokes. She was able to trace it back to my shotgun misfiring. The impact had damaged the artery lining, and it took a while, but it finally tore away from the artery wall, causing the first two strokes. The larger piece then broke off, causing a massive stroke. She had seen similar instances in an area where recreational shooting and hunting were prevalent. She told me I was very lucky as the people she'd treated often died. She also told me I could never fire a shotgun or rifle again. I teared up. That was my new hobby; I was getting good at it! She explained that once I'd shown a proclivity for an artery dissection, it could happen again, and I would need to refrain from anything that could cause impact and injury to my head and neck. No more roller coasters. No more trap and skeet shooting.

It was a small trade-off to be alive.

OCTOBER 8

I still didn't have much internal dialogue. Thoughts were few and far between. My neck ached to the point that I couldn't turn it. I felt fragile, like a raw egg, susceptible to being cracked. All movements were slow and deliberate. I continued to sleep most of the day.

The doctors agreed surgery wouldn't be necessary, and after four days of being in the ICU, the insurance carrier determined I was no longer worthy of care; therefore, the doctors had no choice but to release me. They were apologetic as they told me I could still have another stroke. It wasn't that I was out of the woods, they said; it's possible I could have another stroke, but the possibility was less than it was at the beginning of the week, so there was nothing more they could do for me. They warned me to avoid pepper because even a sneeze could cause more of the artery lining to break off, causing another stroke. They told me I was restricted from driving and advised me to avoid situations where someone could bump into me. I already felt vulnerable, but hearing those things made me feel terrified of movement.

I was moved into an ordinary room on another wing, so I no longer had two dedicated nurses. The strokes made me light-sensitive, and I no longer had the comfort of the darkened ICU room. Compared to the billowy softness of the ICU bed, this bed felt like a piece of plywood. The pillow was even worse. I had left a pillow that cradled my sore neck, and now I had the thinnest excuse for a pillow I'd ever experienced. My discomfort increased minute by minute.

The nurse who came at night for blood work was less skilled than the ICU nurses. His blood draw was painful. Light seeped into the room all night, preventing rest, which fueled my frustration. I couldn't sleep, and I felt as though I'd been abandoned. For the first time all week, I cried.

OCTOBER 9

Post strokes, I could barely tolerate light, and I couldn't tolerate noise— at all. I moved gingerly because I was weak, and my neck hurt. I had been instructed to avoid any sudden movement. Unlike the ICU staff, who kept the lights and their voices low, I was reminded that nobody cared about my sensitivities in this hospital wing. An overly enthusiastic young nurse with curiously dilated pupils bounded into my room to tell me I was being discharged. She didn't know anything about me or my case and couldn't answer any questions; she was simply there to direct me to call for my ride.

I called Joe to pick me up. He told me he wouldn't. I was stunned. He hadn't seen me in four days. He hadn't even visited me in the ICU. This was my husband. My mind reeled. "But how will I get home? I need you to take me home. I don't have a way home." I pleaded.

I don't remember the excuses he rattled off, but they were as fast and eloquent as all his excuses ever were. I called my mother-in-law. She said she would pick me up. Feeling relieved, I thanked her and told her I would call her as soon as I knew the timeframe since I didn't want to waste her time waiting at the hospital.

A couple of hours later, I received a phone call from my sister-in-law (Joe's oldest sister), letting me know that her mother would *not* pick me up. She offered to swing by with the minivan of her kids and their friends. I didn't understand why my mother-in-law backed out. She drove much longer distances all the time for her family. It was unlike her to say yes and then renege. It was also unusual to have her daughter speak for her – that hadn't happened before. I couldn't understand how my sister-in-law thought picking me up with multiple grade school kids in her car was helping, given my fragile and overly sensitive state. I was petrified of being jarred when I'd just been told to avoid situations where sudden movement could lead to another stroke.

After a week of being doted on and cared for so respectfully, I was catapulted right back to the reality of my life and all of the dysfunction. My heart sank. I was defeated. My own family hadn't bothered to visit me, which earlier in the week I had excused because it was out of state. But now, this felt like my entire family had deserted me.

Exhausted from no sleep, emotionally drained from the events of the past week, and now with this outright feeling of abandonment . . . I broke down in sobs.

I was alone. So alone.

It was a Friday. My friends at the time were working, and it seemed too big of an ask, so I called my retired neighbors. Thank God they were willing to pick me up.

Feeling dejected and utterly discarded by everyone related to me, I sat on the edge of my hospital bed, hunched over at the realization that I was reaping the consequences of my husband's alcoholism. The fallout was spilling over onto me so much that everyone was not only finished with him but also with me. If I didn't make a change, my life would only get worse. I would spend the next 40 years alone, and I would continue to be collateral damage to his disgusting behavior.

I had to get out.

That was the most my brain had processed all week. I couldn't even think about what that could look like.

My neighbors drove me home. I slept.

CHAPTER 3
THE NECKLACE

A stroke is a significant trauma to the brain. I had three of them. My body had a lot of healing to do.

I had to occupy myself for the few hours I was awake each day. I loved to read, but it put pressure on my neck, and there was no comfortable position. So, instead, I watched TV. The problem was that volume fluctuations were intolerable as I was so sensitive to noise. HGTV was the only channel that seemed to regulate its programming volume levels with the volume of the commercials. I crocheted and watched TV. I would get what I called "brain pain" inside my head that certainly felt like it was in my brain tissue. I learned that crocheting alleviated that pain. I'm sure there's science behind that somewhere, but if there isn't, there should be. It worked every time.

After an hour or two awake, exhaustion would set back in, and I would go back to sleep.

For the next few weeks, I relied on my neighbors and friends to drive me around and help since Joe insisted on staying at our out-of-state vacation home and refused to be around me. When I was finally cleared to drive six weeks after the accident, I drove for an hour to see my husband, even though the trip hurt my neck and was exhausting.

The last time I was at our second home (the weekend of the gun club event), I had stopped at a small jewelry store. I spotted a beautiful necklace I wanted to buy. I had told Joe about it. I had planned on stopping in the very next weekend to buy it. It was a white gold butterfly with diamonds on one half. I love jewelry, and it was one of those pieces that jumped out at me. I had never seen anything like it, it was gorgeous! I knew jewelry, and it was a fantastic price.

Joe and I talked about my miracle of surviving during a phone conversation while I was in the hospital that first weekend. After experiencing something so traumatic, some materialistic side of me wanted that necklace to symbolize another chance in life. And what would be more perfect than a butterfly? We discussed how the butterfly perfectly represented my new chance at life. Hadn't I seen it the very weekend of the accident? Surely, it was meant to be! I got the impression he would buy it for me, which made me happy.

This would be the first time I had seen Joe since they air-lifted me from the first hospital. I tried to talk him into driving to our home to visit me, but he insisted I drive to him. He persuaded me, as he always did, to do things his way. He further enticed me by saying he had something to show me. He was excited but unusually coy.

Had he picked up the necklace? I wondered. He persisted in telling me to visit. I acquiesced and made the drive.

Joe told me to take my time and stop by the jewelry store, and of course, I did. It was gone. When I asked about the butterfly necklace, the owner said a man had just bought it for his wife. My heart skipped a little. Oh, my goodness, I couldn't wait! He had said he wanted to show me something if I drove up that weekend!

He was cagey because he wanted me to think it was gone when he bought it for me! I was so excited! I couldn't drive fast enough!

I pulled into the drive and saw a large hunting stand on stilts. Surely, that wasn't what he wanted to show me. "Don't be silly, he was excited on the phone, the necklace was purchased . . ." I said to soothe myself from the little bit of dread I felt creeping in.

That day was the second most devastating day since the day in the hospital.

No necklace.

No gift.

He proudly announced that he had gotten a deal on the hunting stand. He bragged about how cheap it was for this local guy to build it for him. (It cost three times the amount of the necklace!) I think part of me went numb. When I expressed my disappointment, he said, "You should go have them order you one." No emotion. No apologies, but gee, wasn't his hunting stand fantastic?

This is how manipulators keep manipulating. This is their sick cycle of abuse. Misdirection, convoluted language, and double-speak. It's like a predator stalking its prey. They know how their target thinks and how to keep their language vague; they know how their victim will interpret things, and they purposely don't clarify.

He knew I wanted the necklace. He knew how to get me to make the drive that weekend.

They string us along. We hope things will get better. We hope they'll change. We hope that one day . . .

It doesn't.

They don't.

It never does.

CHAPTER 4
THE DARKNESS

(Three years earlier)

The weekend binge drinking during the first few years of our marriage had given way to drinking almost every day. There were bouts of sobriety in between, which would lull me into thinking everything was fine. After all, I continued to pray, and I was not going to give up. Surely, that counted for something.

However, by this point, Joe was drinking daily. He was still employed and still traveled frequently for his job. Things on the outside seemed normal, but life at home was becoming weirder and weirder. Oddly, it had not yet become unbearable for me.

I don't remember exactly when he stopped going to church with me out of preference for staying home so he could drink beer while watching church TV. What he watched, of course, was a program where everyone was good, and you didn't need to do anything but bask in your goodness. Not a word about repentance or obedience, but boy, did you feel happy afterward. It was like one of those soccer games where every kid gets a participation trophy. That's not the Gospel of Jesus Christ, but in this stage of the marriage, I had grown tired of going to church by myself, so I stayed home and watched with him.

I wasn't spiritually fed, and I missed the fellowship. I knew better than to pretend this was the Biblical definition of church, but I justified it by saying that at least we were watching together.

My current employer underutilized me; frankly, I was bored beyond belief. It was only a matter of time before new management would swoop in and cut my role. With no kids, my work was my life, and I wanted to be productive. I needed to be productive. I had an interview with a new company to be a product manager. This new job would offer me an extraordinary opportunity to level up my career. Before the interview, Joe and I discussed a fair salary for this type of role and what I should ask for in a compensation package.

When I received the offer, it was exactly what I had asked for, which was thrilling! It was great to be wanted and viewed as worthy of what I asked for instead of feeling like I had to settle. I accepted the offer because Joe was on a business trip, and I couldn't reach him. I felt proud and energized with the anticipation of a new position, company, and possibilities.

The next day, Joe returned home, and even though I had told him I took the job over the phone, it somehow took hours and a lot of beer to spur him into asshole gear before he reacted.

I was sitting cross-legged on the floor in my room watching TV when suddenly, he became unhinged and started yelling from the living room. He stormed down the hall to the doorway of my room. He was irate that I had accepted the job without asking him first. Bewildered by his delayed reaction and the idea that I needed his permission, I reminded him that we had discussed everything ahead of time, and the company had offered me exactly what he and I had agreed to ask for. What more was there to discuss? Why would I delay accepting?

I was dumbfounded. He had never acted this way about anything work-related before. As prestige-driven as he was, and for all his emphasis on money, I was genuinely surprised he was mad. He had always encouraged any effort or time I spent on my career. The idea that I had to wait for his blessing before a decision like this was a disturbing new development.

I learned that when someone rages, all logic goes out the window. They are inconsolable. Good points aren't enough. He was livid. I hadn't waited for him or asked for his permission.

The self-centeredness and irrational behavior weren't new, but the level of intensity that it had reached certainly was. He stood outside my room spewing hate-filled words, including the one word every woman despises, unless one is British because it is only ever used in the most demeaning and derogatory way. He even threatened divorce. Divorce! All because I didn't ask his permission to accept the job. He had yelled *at* me before. He had said plenty of unkind things over the years. He had been hurtful. But he had never called me names before. This was a new low.

I sat there frozen. I didn't know quite what to do or how to respond.

And then I felt it.

A shadow appeared immediately behind my left shoulder, and I experienced what felt like hot breath on the left side of my neck. It moved behind me. Not daring to enrage Joe further but recognizing the spiritual nature of the darkness, I whispered, "Get behind me, Satan." As quickly as the shadow had come, it was gone. I was terrified. But with those words, the threatening presence left.

Joe turned and stomped back to the living room. I shut my bedroom door and sat there, trying to process what I had just experienced.

Things only got worse. He established new rules for the house, assigning certain light switches that he would use and certain switches I was allowed to use—all under the guise of avoiding germs. I would constantly navigate a dark house, and on the occasion when I was brazen enough to use "his" light switch, I would endure his tantrum and be forced to listen to him rage on and on about how selfish I was.

I complied to keep the peace.

The control was so ingrained that even when he wasn't home, I would adhere to his rules for fear of disrespecting his wishes or because I would feel guilty for violating the agreement not to touch them. When I used those light switches, I did so with a twinge of guilt, as if I was doing something morally wrong.

As time passed, I felt a sense of defiance just by using a light switch. That was probably the start of healthy emotions.

This is how abuse starts and proliferates. It starts with small things and becomes more significant. For the abuser, it's a sickness that needs to control every aspect of life, no matter how small or how much pain, suffering, or inconvenience it will cause their victim. These are things that people in healthy situations don't even think about. But those of us in abusive environments learn to navigate to avoid the volatile emotional landmines. We constantly try to guess the mood, avoid the triggers, and subjugate ourselves to the abuser's every whim.

We are constantly watched.

We are constantly judged.

Compliance is required. Any act, however small, perceived as defiance will be punished.

We are not allowed to be tired, to slip up, or to have a bad day. If we claim we're tired, we're accused of being disobedient. If we claim to have "not been thinking," we're accused of being selfish or stupid.

There is no grace. Everything is on the abuser's terms, and he/she is always right. If you try to speak up, stand up for yourself, or point out how just this one time you might have a valid point, the abuser will wear you down with manipulation until you either agree or end up believing he/she is right – once again.

In severely abusive relationships, the victim is always wrong. Case closed.

I suppose we all comply for different reasons. My reasons were to avoid being screamed at so that I could have a "normal" day. In my compliance, I became a willing participant in the great charade. I was fooling myself into thinking I could have something that resembled normal, so I continued playing into Joe's grand scheme of being the master of his universe.

Looking back, the emotional control he had over me was so unreal, it's laughable – except that it isn't. Over the next few years, I never knew what I'd find when I got home after work. Pulling up to the garage produced a pit in my stomach. When the garage door opened, revealing he was at our vacation home, I felt enormous relief and could enjoy a quiet, peaceful evening. When his truck was there, I'd brace myself for what might come next. If he were passed out on the couch, I would tiptoe around the dark house, make dinner, creep into my room to eat, and watch TV. I learned to turn my light off if I heard him stir because if my light was off, he wouldn't bother me. I would then wait until he went back to sleep before I turned my light back on or ventured out of my room.

Two more years passed like this. Night after night, I would make dinner for myself and take it to my room.

I prayed for him to get better. He only got worse.

He had blackout rages. One event that particularly frightened me was when he went off on a tirade about me doing something to him that had happened to a friend. How was his brain taking something that happened to someone else 15 years ago and morphing it into his own experience now? That diversion from reality was scary. The next day, he didn't remember any of it. At least, that's what he told me.

His diet consisted of fatty, fried bar food and beer. I didn't see him eat any real food or drink water. He had withered away, and his belly had become distended, which I suspected was due to a nutrition deficit. His tantrums and verbal assaults were larger than he was, and that's how he kept his hold on me. His mean spirit was so much bigger than his physical presence. Over the years, I gave in, little by little, so that it became my default programming.

I prayed for him to die.

He didn't.

With every passing year, I became increasingly isolated and lost more and more of myself.

By now, he started at 8 am with a "breakfast beer" and would drink throughout the day until he fell asleep or passed out. I was never quite sure which it was.

His favorite beer came not just in a case of 24 but in a pack of 30, and he was drinking the entire case, or more, a day with the occasional stiff drink thrown in. It's incredible what the human body can endure. By this time, I had finally allowed myself to admit I was married to an alcoholic. For years, I had known but had quickly dismissed the thought of it, too afraid to face all that word entailed.

When I was home alone, I would say the previously unspeakable words out loud. Hearing "My husband is an alcoholic" pour out of my mouth was strange and unsavory. It was a practice of sorts to the big reveal and having to answer questions. "It's been a gradual progression." I would say to no one. I was rehearsing the words of someone I didn't want to be: a weak person propping up a secret that was destroying our lives.

I attended the little country church close to our vacation spot one Sunday. The sermon included a news story about a young boy attacked by an alligator. While the alligator clamped down on the boy's legs, his mother grabbed the boy's arms and held on to him, unwilling to relinquish him to the predator. Afterward, when the little boy was asked to show off the scars on his legs, he also boasted about the scars on his arms because they proved how much his mother loved him because she refused to let go.

The idea that those who love us sometimes hurt us in their attempt to help us hit home. Scars are sometimes necessary. I couldn't just watch Joe be taken out by alcohol. I had to hold on. I didn't know what more I could do, but I wasn't ready to walk away. I left the service convinced I had to *do* something. I couldn't live like this anymore. He would die if I didn't do anything. Even if I hurt him in the process, wouldn't the pain be worth it if it saved his life?

That week, I tried one more time to bring up his drinking. He refused to discuss any "problem" but said he would never go anywhere for help locally because he wouldn't want people to know. It was the first glimmer of an admission I'd ever received! He shut down the discussion after that one sentence.

Only a few weeks later, he lost his job. He had been drinking 16 hours a day and consuming 30 to 45 beers a day for a long stretch by this point, so I'm pretty sure someone at his work had noticed. He could no longer use "missing work" as an excuse to not get help. I started researching options. I found someone to help me do an intervention and then escort him to a rehab facility. I knew Joe would never forgive me if I dared tell his friends about it, but I wasn't sure if he'd forgive me for telling his family either. I also knew I couldn't pull this off by myself.

So, I called his family. I came clean about their son and brother. They all had some awareness but no idea how bad things were. He had kept them at arm's length for a reason. I told them I had tried everything. He refused help, refused to talk about it, and refused to admit there was a problem.

As we plotted and the big day loomed closer, I began losing my resolve. On my lunch break one day, I drove to a fast-food parking lot and pulled back by the dumpster where I hoped no one would see and I cried until my eyes were practically swollen shut. I cried harder than I had ever cried before. It was a mourning of all those dreams of a loving husband, a godly marriage, a man who would love me, a man I could respect. It was as if my soul were wringing out every drop of grief I had experienced over the past decade.

Joe was fiercely private. I feared he would never forgive me for divulging this secret to his family, for breaking his trust. His facade would be forever shattered. I knew on a cellular level that things would never be the same. Perhaps, given enough time, he would view the scars of betrayal as part of his recovery story, just like that story of the little boy and the alligator. Surely, he would see I was saving him from the evil forces trying to take him out. I wasn't convinced of that, but by this point, I couldn't focus on it. I had enabled his addiction, and I felt that I had to do something before he drank himself to death. I felt I had no choice because the blackout rages were playing with the edges of insanity. I feared for my life.

I needed someone I trusted to tell me whether I was doing the right thing. I called my uncle. He assured me I was doing the right thing. After gathering myself, I returned to work and talked to my boss. I figured he'd need to know so he didn't take my emotions or lack of focus as performance-related or lack of initiative. I couldn't risk losing my job. I needed stability, and since Joe wasn't working, we needed the income. My boss was amazingly understanding. A few days later, he handed me the business card of a counselor.

With Joe's family supporting me, we moved forward with the gross and dramatic intervention and sent him to an out-of-state drug and alcohol recovery center. Because they didn't want an alcoholic to go into detox without medical supervision, they allowed Joe to drink the entire flight. Bob, the interventionist who accompanied him, told me he had never seen anyone drink so much. I sighed, "Welcome to my world." I felt a strange sense of comfort. For the first time, I heard someone tell me they were experienced in this sort of thing, and this was, indeed, really, *really,* bad.

The rehab facility checked him in, ran medical tests, and called me and told me they'd never seen someone with blood alcohol levels that high . . . still alive.

Another stamp of validation that I had made the right choice to seek help.

CHAPTER 5
THE MEETINGS

When I thought about my future, it had been normal for me to visualize how different scenarios could play out. I would envision myself achieving the goal, enjoying that vacation, etc. Whatever my circumstances, there had always been some path forward, an almost cinematic view of possibilities. This time, it was different. When I tried to focus on what would be next, there was nothing but blackness—a void. It terrified me.

I started counseling because the rehab center had told me I needed it. My counselor started telling me my life was not "normal". At one point she said, "Leah, that's abusive behavior." I had never thought of myself as a victim, much less a victim of abuse. This was new information for me to process, and it was hard for me to accept. But, little by little the truth started causing the walls to fall on this dark world that Joe had constructed around me. It was during those sessions that I started learning about what manipulation and control looked like. For the first time, I was beginning to understand I was being emotionally and psychologically abused.

The next 28 days were surreal. Joe called and cried and begged to come home. He would relay how awful it was and how he was not like the rest of the people in the program. He whined that they made him clean the kitchen and bathrooms, tasks he found beneath him. I remember I couldn't suppress a smile. After all these years of doing all that type of work for him, I had little sympathy for that grievance. It was the start of my being able to process authentic and healthy emotions in a situation. Instead of trying to fix it for him and enable and do it for him, I was acutely aware that his behavior had caused all of this. It was nice hearing him experience some discomfort because of his actions. Why should I feel sorry for him when he caused me so much pain all these years? It was only by having him physically removed that allowed me, for the first time, to start seeing things more objectively. I was beginning to not twist myself into a pretzel to accommodate his every emotional whim. The fact that he now felt sad, discouraged, and scared – felt fair.

I continued to pray, so I assumed I would get my miracle. I was certain he would have some breakthrough and be relieved to know he could live without the alcohol. As the weeks of rehab wore on, however, something else entirely was revealed. Without the alcohol, he had no tolerance for me. He didn't treat me as a wife or a partner, much less a child of God. He spoke to me as if I were his servant, one who was paid to wait on him hand and foot. At first, he was sweet and tried to convince me to let him come home while promising many things. When I refused repeatedly to let him come home without completing the program, he became openly defiant and demeaning. The mean and controlling man, no longer weakened by alcohol, was now becoming strong. Was this who he was? Perhaps it was the alcohol all those years that had tempered his aggression and hatred toward me? Sobriety wasn't looking like I thought it would.

Toward the end of the program, his primary counselor called me and said she felt she had experienced a breakthrough with him. I was at work and slipped into a conference room for privacy. She excitedly relayed that he broke down and cried as he explained when his company had gone through its major cutback, he had to let 45 people go, and that's when he let his drinking get the better of him. Letting all those people go crushed him. She went on to say that she could understand and sympathize with him on how that was a reasonable trigger that could cause something to change one's behavior drastically. She was audibly relieved by this new information.

My blood ran cold.

He was the only employee who was let go that day. He didn't have anyone reporting to him. He didn't have to fire anyone, much less 45 people! I had to explain to her that none of that was true. It was her turn to be quiet. Here she was, an experienced drug and alcohol addiction counselor, and she, too, had fallen for his deception.

Once again, I felt a strange validation. I wasn't the only one he had duped. I wasn't as stupid as he had made me feel all those years. Learning that a seasoned professional had also fallen for his lies gave me a sense of satisfaction.

Ever since I had sent Joe off to rehab and gone into counseling, I had attended Al-Anon meetings. I don't even remember if someone recommended it or if I started going because I thought it was what I was supposed to do. Maybe it was just the cultural expectation: Have an alcoholic in your family? Join Al-Anon. The intention was good. We often recommend things to people we haven't personally experienced because we don't know what else to do. And sometimes, we do something because it feels like doing something is better than doing nothing.

It was a frigid November. I remember it was one of those Midwest winter nights when the metal in cars creaked, and even the ground seemed to groan. I've always thought of that as the inanimate world in a unanimous complaint with us against the frozen air. I pulled my coat more tightly around me to fend off the biting wind as I walked from my car past the group of shivering smokers into the building.

Unfortunately, the only meetings in my area were held at an old, run-down school-turned-community-center in one of the roughest areas of town. It was not a welcome place for a corporately dressed woman in high heels. To say I stood out would be an understatement.

There were unfriendly stares. I didn't fit in. I should have just returned to my car. But I have never been one to cave to peer pressure; I've always just forged ahead – and so I did in this situation. This is where my life had taken me, and I needed help too. Let them stare. I was here to get better, and this was where people like me were supposed to go, so I sucked it up as part of the penance for my life falling to this level.

I was expecting a warm greeting—possibly even an overly friendly, sweet, older woman offering me coffee and doughnuts as I learned to navigate this new world of "meetings."

Except this wasn't Hollywood.
No coffee.
No doughnuts.
No welcome.
No warmth.

The basement classroom where my group met only had half the fluorescent lights working, and at least one buzzed and flickered incessantly. In combination with the 1950s psychiatric ward-like mint green paint color, old chairs, and broken tiles, it would have made the perfect setting for some asylum horror flick.

A welcome place to get help? Not so much.

During these meetings, the women shared gruesome tales. We would commiserate with platitudes like "Oh, how awful," "I'm so sorry," and the like. I remember sitting there frustrated because there was never a path forward. These women had no hope, and they had been coming for years! It was as if embracing that they were "powerless" had rendered them action-less.

How would I possibly find hope? Hearing and repeating a message of powerlessness doesn't inspire encouragement or any forward motion. It can become an excuse for passivity, and it is another one of Satan's lies to keep us perpetuating the sin cycle. He would have us believe there is nothing more.

I'll never forget my last meeting, the final straw, as it were. Joe was coming home from rehab later that week. I was excited to see him. It had been an excruciatingly long four weeks, and when it was my turn to share with the group, I shared my hopefulness with these beleaguered women, expecting encouragement. That night, an addict joined our group because she had children who were addicts. Previously, she had been very quiet, but after I spoke, her face twisted with ugliness and rage as she leaned close to my face and snarled, almost gleefully, "He'll never change. He won't change until he's ready to change!"

Her face changed momentarily as the darkness flitted across it. I was stunned. This group was non-confrontational and passive. Everyone nodded in agreement and understanding as we shared hardships week in and week out. No one ever attacked a fellow member - until that night.

So much for hope. So much for support.

No one said a word. Everyone was as startled as I was by her outburst. I was so taken aback by and unnerved by aggressiveness that my hands started shaking. I made it to my car, collapsed in my seat, and cried uncontrollably. I beat my fists so hard on the steering wheel I thought it might break. Years of heartache and pain had finally turned into anger.

The humiliation, hopelessness, disappointment, darkness—all the rage that had been building up inside—all of it came out, and somewhere in that meltdown came the thought that changed everything.

It was that quiet voice of the Holy Spirit whispering. That inner nudging revealed I *did* have the ability to say no, to say I was no longer going to stay in spiritual bondage. That inner prompting suggested that even though Satan had laid claim to my husband, I had a choice to be free.

That little spark of hope illuminated something deep within that desired healing. It was a seed of hope in the darkness, the hope that defied logic and circumstance, that defiant hope that wanted what God wanted for me - nothing less than the fullness of Himself.

In those moments, I knew I could never return to the meetings. I had tried, and they had failed me. I rejected what the world, culture, and what others said. That was not the way forward. I wasn't sure what it would look like. But I knew I wasn't finding the truth at those meetings.

What I needed was not inside the depressing community building with the beaten down, stuck women who, for decades, came to the same meeting, said the same thing, and lived the same life year after year, decade after decade.

For those women, nothing ever changed. Nothing.

That would not be my story. The Holy Spirit was whispering to me. He was whispering there was more, and I felt that truth in every cell of my body. There *was* more. I did have a choice. I had the power to change my situation, stand up to lies, deceit, and abuse, say, "No more," and turn toward my Jesus for the whole truth.

When "higher power" means nothing more to you than some words in a book, you will stay stuck. And miserable. And destined to relive the same bad patterns of behavior repeatedly. If you believe in the God of the Bible but minimize him and stuff him into the culturally accepted "higher power" box to remain in a group or be accepted by man, you will not only miss out on the blessing that comes with praise and worship, but you are in danger of not knowing Him at all.

If you remove God from the equation, all you're left with is humanity – broken humanity. If you have God in your life, you do not need to scrape the bottom of the barrel with what the culture offers and what others are all too eager to accept. As a believer in Christ Jesus, you have more options. Jesus offers more. Learn to expect more.

Desire more!

What good does it do for me to dilute the one thing powerful enough to give me any hope? A watered-down gospel undermines the authority of an Almighty God. A watered-down view of God will weaken our relationship with Him. A watered-down faith doesn't have the kind of healing power that I needed. And a watered-down recovery process will be no recovery at all.

If you live in an area with a vibrant group of Al-Anon members, it may be just what you need. Attend. Participate! For some, these groups are absolute lifelines. For me, however, I needed the full power of Jesus and a place where I could confess His name openly.

CHAPTER 6

THE LOOK

The long-anticipated day came. The month-long rehab program ended, and Joe called with the time his flight would arrive and asked that I pick him up instead of making him take the bus.

Of course! Of course, I would! He had gone through rehab. I was so proud of him! Despite the conversation with his counselor, despite sensing his anger on the phone, I was still hopeful. I have heard stories throughout my life of overcoming alcoholism, and men thanked their wives for helping them and their families for sticking by them. I had been praying, so I was hoping now that he was coming home that there would be that same humility and acknowledgment of what he had done to our marriage, to himself, and to me. I expected gratitude for getting him into the program. I was looking forward to future possibilities, ready to forgive it all and start a new chapter. This is what I had been begging God for – *for years*!

I desperately wanted his love, his adoration, and a healthy marriage. I had told God many times I would give up everything to have him healthy, so I couldn't wait to see him sober. I was excited and emotional and almost giddy with anticipation of his homecoming. I pulled up to the terminal and saw him with pink, full cheeks, and he'd grown out his beard. It was a relief to no longer see the emaciated man he had been. I couldn't help but think about our new life and what a fabulous story of recovery he would have! If only I could receive some hint of love from him . . . I was still on edge but was ardently hopeful.

Then he locked eyes with me and there was no humility or love. He glared at me. There was a cold, distance that had never been there before.

His hatred pierced me.

He had been angry with me plenty of times, but never, ever had I seen such contempt in his eyes. My heart lurched and then sank into a pit of sadness.

I felt sick.

He was not grateful. He was resentful.

Within 30 days, he was drinking again.

CHAPTER 7
THE DECISION

[Back to the months after the strokes]

As soon as my short-term disability timeframe was up, I went back to work. I should've delayed going back to work so soon, but Joe never looked for work after losing his job. Since the hospital stay cost well over $100K, and I would continue to have follow-up care, I had to keep my job to keep my insurance, so I pushed myself to my limit.

My job at the time consisted of co-workers and management who were incredibly compassionate and understanding about my situation. They were more concerned about what had happened to me and rejoiced more when I returned to work than any of my family members. Throughout my marriage, I had thrown myself into work because it was where I had peace. It was my sense of normal. It was the area of my life I could somewhat control. I was free to be me. Work was my haven.

And I could touch any light switch I wanted to.

Before my strokes, I never had to search for the right word when writing and could type fast. I used to be so focused someone could call my name, and I wouldn't hear them. But now, back at work, everyday things were challenging. I had to stop and think if I should type "their" or "there." Instead of proofreading once, I needed to reread multiple times to catch errors. Mid-sentence I would pause to search for the appropriate word. It was incredibly frustrating.

Not only did I struggle with selecting the right words, but I also couldn't focus. I'd be working at the computer, but my mind would find the conversation on the other side of the office much more interesting. It was a strange sensation, but it felt like my brain waves were walking over to join the dialogue. It didn't matter how much I tried to ignore it. I wondered if this is what those with ADHD experienced. No matter what I tried, I could not force myself to concentrate. Would I ever be able to function the way I used to? Would I ever be able to focus again? Would I eventually lose my job when they discovered I had lost all this cognitive ability?

I was terrified and that stress exhausted me more.

God still provided. Everyone at work understood I had a great deal of recovery ahead and they offered me more grace than I gave myself. They gave me the freedom to leave when I was exhausted. They allowed me time to heal. Even after being cleared for air travel, they let me travel on my schedule, understanding that I would require more sleep and miss out on some meetings and activities. They knew my character, I was doing my best, and they were happy to have me with them.

Their compassion was in stark contrast to my family's lack of empathy. That was another layer of truth being revealed. It was also a way that God showed me mercy through others. I wouldn't find out until later, but the people at my company had become aware of my husband's drinking. They understood I was dealing with more than physical pain and stroke recovery. They showed me the kindness and compassion I desperately needed.

Experiencing physical recovery alone strengthened my mind. Being out from under the constant gaslighting, I was able to see more clearly. I had been brainwashed. I was clinging to a legal definition of marriage, but my husband had abdicated his role. I was in a two-party union alone. I was being faithful to someone who wasn't faithful to me.

Even though I mourned my lack of a marital relationship and hated that my husband wasn't at our home to take care of me, that period of solitude provided me with the space to realize just how much I did and how very little he did.

The veil of deceit was slowly being peeled away. I started noticing the lies. It was a time of revelation. I knew I wanted out; I knew I needed out, but I didn't know how I would get out.

It was about five months after the strokes that I, again, drove to visit Joe at our vacation home. I found a cooler in the pantry filled with empty beer cans, and he had the audacity to stand one foot away from me and look at me with those puppy dog eyes and tell me he hadn't been drinking, and the beer "wasn't his."

Another wave of cold reality hit me.

The masterful lies he told to the therapist at rehab and now this. I had been separated from him long enough by now that I could see the world more clearly. This time, I knew it was a lie. I could see the empty beer cans and that he had even attempted to hide them. But he *seemed* truthful. I stood there staring at him, my mind racing between the evidence and his words. And that's how I had stayed in the dark for so many years. The lie was prettier than the truth.

He had me completely gaslighted. I could stare at evidence to the contrary and *still* be bamboozled by him. How many times had this happened? How many other things had he said over the years with that same sincere look? I knew how that counselor was duped - the same way he had deceived me all those years – carefully crafted lies backed with the most honest and sincere tone and look.

Joe had presented himself as one thing, agreed with me, drew from me, and hid his true identity. He presented as the person I would accept. I took him at face value. I always had. I had believed everything. But now I was realizing there was so much more to the story. There was more to my marriage, to the man I had married, that I didn't know. Just how many lies had I believed over the years? With the veil torn, I started sensing I could be in danger. It became clear that I was dealing with something darker than I had ever wanted to acknowledge.

I didn't see it at the time, but years later, I was overwhelmed by the memories of bizarre situations with women. Each instance carried, at a minimum, indecency, and betrayal. However, I'll never know the degree of infidelity. To every one of my questions, he would respond with statements telling me I was being irrational, insecure, or jealous. He wore me down with detailed explanations and rationalizations. He always turned the focus of the argument back to me. He could twist any action of his into a character judgment on me. He wouldn't relent, and with no hard evidence, I would give up because when I accepted his view, he was calm and happy. I didn't want discord. I liked peace, so I dismissed one comment and occurrence at a time.

I didn't want to believe the man I married was anything other than what I wanted him to be. It was so much easier to believe the lie.

As I've shared these and other stories over the years, I've seen the look in others' eyes—the look that says, "You poor soul" or, "How could you not see it?" I had to admit what I ignored and come to terms with what I tolerated. That is not a person I want to acknowledge that I once was. But that is who I was, and I've had to forgive myself.

This is why my heart aches for women in, or coming out of, abusive situations. Truth has been turned upside down and used against us. Our emotions are so manipulated that they become unregulated and unreliable as a source of intuition. Our very sense of self is broken.

We are not victims in the sense that we are completely powerless, but we have allowed our power to be stripped. Healing can begin only when we have the clarity to see around us and recognize that we can take our power back.

Freedom isn't a thing given to us, it's something to be exercised. When we're in these hyper-controlled relationships, it isn't that we have been physically robbed of freedom, but we have been convinced to believe we can't make good choices and that our will should always align with our abuser's. The perpetrator will beat us down emotionally, if not physically, to the point of giving in and giving up, but that freedom is still there for the taking.

Once we have the eyes to see, it's a matter of reaching out and grasping hold of that freedom to choose, the freedom to leave, or simply the freedom to think for ourselves, especially if we stay.

A few more months passed, but Joe still wasn't working. I was shouldering the entire financial burden as well as taking care of the house, yard, and cars and paying the bills. The stress was taking a toll. I started to experience stroke symptoms again.

It was one of those hot, muggy Midwest July days that makes breathing difficult for a healthy person. It was the kind of day sensible people determine is too hot and humid for any strenuous outdoor activity. Unless, of course, you're not the one doing it.

Joe insisted I mow the side lawn. Because it was too narrow for the riding lawn mower, it meant using the push mower. I didn't feel well, and stroke symptoms had reappeared. Listening to yet another tantrum wasn't appealing either, so I went outside and started up the mower. I remember that effort alone left me breathless. It was then that I finally had the next level of awareness that his "love" for me was one of convenience only. He loved me when I could do things for him, but he did not care if I lived or died. With tears running down my face, I knew the relationship was over, and I could not continue living like this. If this is how he treated me after a major health crisis and the threat of another one, his priorities were clear, and they certainly didn't include my well-being.

How could I leave? Marriage was forever. How could I leave since God hates divorce? How could I leave when all our friends were his? How would we split assets? How would I start over? The questions made my head hurt. It was all too much.

CHAPTER 8
THE OUT

After a follow-up appointment, the doctors advised me that I was experiencing stress-induced symptoms, which are common side effects of strokes – in old ladies. I made light of it, but it really bothered me that I was experiencing things women thirty years my senior experienced. Besides, my life was the definition of stress. I wasn't sure how to reduce it, much less avoid it.

Things only worsened, solidifying my decision to end the drama that had become my life. It was neither productive nor God-honoring. I prayed. I had asked and begged Joe to talk to me, to get help. I had been faithful. I had never strayed. I had not given up on my marriage or him. I had sacrificed and been submissive to the point of sinning myself as I was caught in covering up his lies.

I had begged and bargained with God for him to get better. Later, I hoped for him to die so that I could be free from the nightmare. I did not give up. I wouldn't give up. And one day, in my mind, I heard, "You did everything I asked you to do."

And with that, I realized it was time for me to leave; otherwise, I would die under the soul-crushing weight of the abuse.

I had enabled him, and if I stayed and continued to enable him, he would likely drink himself to death. Perhaps, if I finally left, he would hit that "rock bottom" everyone says is necessary before recovery. My job allowed him to remain unemployed and maintain his lifestyle. My leaving was the only hope either of us had for a future.

The next two months were spent in quiet reflection. I finally called my mom. I knew I wouldn't go back on my word once I told her I was leaving, so I used her to hold myself accountable. My mom responded, "I thought you'd never leave."

I contacted an attorney.

The tables had turned. All the years of Joe putting more and more burdens on me now meant I had control of the credit cards and the bank accounts. Everything was in my control.

Finally, I had a way out.

It wasn't easy. It was a taxing process. For Christians who take the vow of marriage seriously, divorce feels like a ripping out of your soul. I don't wish it on my enemies. I did feel a spiritual kind of tear occurring. Was it the covenant bonds of marriage being ruptured, or was it the ripping free of the spiritual bondage I was in? To this day, I don't know. But I do know that God does not leave us in the muck.

Even when we've voluntarily stayed in it for years.

Even when we've created it ourselves.

Even when the muck is all we know.

When we cry out to Him.

When we lay our lives at His feet.

When we welcome His whole presence to come into our lives. He does come to us, and He will make His presence known.

CHAPTER 9
THE ESCAPE

My life had been drained out of me. I stayed until I thought I would die if I didn't get out. I gave him more money than I needed to. I left more furniture and household items than I should have. I caved to every demand so that he would just sign the papers. In a sense, I was buying my freedom. I realized I had stayed foolishly long. At this point, I needed to get out and be finished.

Memories from early in the marriage flooded my mind like the time he had dinner with an ex-girlfriend one week before our wedding. He got mad at me when I told him it bothered me. On our wedding day, one of Joe's co-workers told me what a beautiful ceremony it was and casually said, "I never knew Joe was so religious." That struck my heart. Anyone who knew me – friend or foe – knew I was a Christian. The day after the wedding, instead of driving with me, he had insisted on riding the hour and a half with his buddy, who had flown in from California. He convinced me it would be rude for him not to ride with the person who flew in. Somehow, it wasn't rude to ignore your wife. It was less than 24 hours after our wedding! I was devastated. But it was too late.

All of those instances that I had shoved down for so long came rushing back, and that reinforced my decision as I realized that I had put up with a degrading husband for far too long.

He did not bother to show up to the courthouse to finalize the divorce. Everyone else in the courtroom getting divorced appeared as indifferent as waiting to get one's driver's license. Couple after couple casually went before the judge. Mostly, they all chatted amiably and looked happy to be getting divorced. For me, it was very emotional. The judge looked curiously at me since I was the one filing, and Joe wasn't there to cause any distress, but still, there I was crying. No one else in the courtroom was crying, but there I was. . . crushed that life had come to this. I was devastated to admit the defeat of divorce and what my life had become.

The moment it was done, the darkness dissipated. A weight was lifted. I walked out of the courthouse and for the first time in 13 ½ years . . . I no longer felt alone.

It was the first day of a new life.

It was odd because I hadn't been consciously aware of being alone because I was so used to it. Even though I had been married for over a decade, I had done so much alone.

Sure, there were exceptions, and certainly, things deteriorated when his drinking escalated, but for most of my life with him, I did things alone. I visited my parents alone and went grocery shopping alone. I went to company parties alone. I slept alone.

I always felt alone. Even when he was in the same house with me, I was alone. But that day, when the court released me from marriage, I felt a cosmic shift. It was a palpable change in my soul, in my metaphysical self. It was a wholeness, completeness . . . a shedding of the dark cloud of oppression and abuse.

SECTION II
HEALING & RESTORATION

CHAPTER 10
DEFIANT HOPE

With what the enemy tries to destroy us, God, in all His goodness, swoops in and harnesses for good. For years, I maintained that my family let me down, but with time comes perspective. Looking back all these years later, I can see that God used all that to peel back the layers of wool over my eyes that concealed the truth.

I am glad I felt abandoned because that was the rock bottom I needed to jar me into the truth of my situation. They were right to enforce their boundaries. Had they taken me home, it would have covered up Joe's lack of empathy and compassion even more, and I would have continued in my delusion even longer.

As the lies began to unravel, I was slowly able to come to terms with reality and see my life for what it was. The truth shall set you free. That Scripture is about Jesus being the truth and the only path to salvation, but it sure applies to everyday things, too.

Acceptance and passivity had brought me to a place of enabling, not delivered me from it. Lying down in defeat is not how battles are won – spiritual or otherwise.

If we no longer want to be a slave in our spiritual bondage, there is a way out, but it isn't by lying low, being passive, and allowing evil to have victory over us and our lives. We must take a stand. We must fight our battles.

David did not approach Goliath waving a white flag. Instead, he went out and faced him head-on with a slingshot and a stone, along with faith that God was fighting with him. David then took swift action using the knowledge and skills God had given him. That is how he slew Goliath and saved the Israelites from becoming Philistine slaves.

Maybe you're like me, who listened to old programming that told me I had no choice in how I was treated, and yet, the Holy Spirit stirs within, suggesting there is more. Perhaps you are like I was and don't want to minimize a Holy God to a "greater power," and you are desperate to live a godly life, and yet, week after week, you're told just to accept things as they are or that there's no way out. You might be hearing that you must be more patient, loving, and forgiving.

How do we justify that stuckness?

How do we grow in that darkness?

As Christians, we can do better. We must do better. There is a counterpoint to what the world offers: immersion in God's word within a community. The answer lies in having a trusted group of Christ-followers with whom you can pray, share, cry, and grow. Whether you stay or leave your relationship, you need community.

The premise that we are powerless is a slippery slope. True, we do not control the world or anyone else's actions. Neither are we responsible for anyone's drinking, addiction, or other behavior. However, that does not mean we have no power at all. We have power over our thoughts. We have power over our actions. As believers in Christ Jesus, we know we are held accountable for both. And here's the best part: we are not left to fend for ourselves.

If you are a Christ follower, you have an indwelling of the Holy Spirit.

> "Do not be anxious about anything, but in every situation, by prayer and petition, with thanksgiving, present your requests to God. ⁷ And the peace of God, which transcends all understanding, will guard your hearts and your minds in Christ Jesus. Finally, brothers and sisters, whatever is true, whatever is noble, whatever is right, whatever is pure, whatever is lovely, whatever is admirable—if anything is excellent or praiseworthy—think about such things." (Phil 4:6-8)

I find the message of "being powerless" counter to scripture because if you look up alternate words for "powerless," you'll see words like impotent, helpless, ineffective, and paralyzed. But if we read Scripture, we find this:

> "I can do all this through him who gives me strength." (Phil 4:13)

God instructs us to pray for strength to endure and for patience. Through the power of the Holy Spirit, we can overcome our sinful thoughts and thwart sinful desires. That is not a message of "powerlessness."

> "The LORD is my strength and my shield; my heart trusts in him, and he helps me. My heart leaps for joy, and with my song I praise him. The LORD is the strength of his people, a fortress of salvation for his anointed one." (Psa 28:7-8)

A watered-down truth of the Gospel neuters our faith. Rote mantras may soothe those of the world who have nothing else to cling to, but we are offered more than that as Christians! The question is, will you listen to the world or a Holy God?

That "support" group I attended was led by untrained, unhealed women who were nothing more than the blind leading the blind in an unending tunnel of despair. Not a single one had any hope to share with anyone else.

Where was the encouragement? I was so disappointed by the lack of hope that it made me angry for myself and all the women there. Some of these ladies had started going in their 20s and were now in their 60s. They were no longer dealing with just a husband who was an addict. but now they were going through the exact same battles with children and grandchildren who were addicts. All because they never exited the cycle.

And so, it goes—generation after generation.

These women came every week for decades—decades! That equates to thousands of hours spent doing nothing to move forward, nothing to grow, nothing that brings joy and goodness, just a constant state of the same—the same despair, the same feeling of helplessness, the same sense of shame.

No wonder our world is so broken.

This is exactly where Satan wants to keep us. Broken. Stuck in darkness. With no genuine fellowship. No hope. No fruit.

I dared to hope for more. Everything in me rejected the notion that I couldn't expect more. I needed more and I *knew* there was more. The Holy Spirit was speaking to me, filling me with hope when the world could offer me none. He breathed life into me even as the world tried to snatch it away. He infused me with a defiant hope that had no logic and no place in my life but for God.

> "May the God of hope fill you with all joy and peace as you trust in him, so that you may overflow with hope by the power of the Holy Spirit." (Rom 15:13)

My heart breaks for women who think of God as just a "higher power" or that their despair is all there is. There is so much more, regardless of whether you stay or leave your situation.

There is light. There is hope. Healing can be yours.

Your power comes from a Holy and omnipotent God. You have been given the ability to make decisions. You *can* end the cycle for yourself. You can choose not to participate. You can opt out, you can exit. You probably can't even begin to fathom what that ripple effect will have on others if you get off the hamster wheel of abuse.

My husband left me in every way a man can leave his wife. I merely filed the paperwork so the state would recognize the dissolution. My story is not your story. Your marriage may indeed be salvageable. Many are. I've worked with women whose brief separation caused their husbands to change behaviors, and still, years later, they are happy and content. They've found a way to move forward with mutual respect and love. Some women have struggled with their own demons. When offered a different perspective than their worldly friends can offer, they were able to open communication with their husbands and make their marriage work.

Some, like me, who didn't have a repentant spouse, got out.

We each have our own path and our own story. You must seek God for the answer to your situation because you won't be the only one who suffers the consequences of that decision.

Regardless of your choice, God still loves you and delights in you. He won't frown on you because you leave, nor will you earn points for staying. We can't earn His love. He gives it freely. Even if you feel far from Him or have stopped attending church, He is just waiting for you to turn toward Him. He's already there.

God offers us a way back to Him. Christ was and is the way back for humanity after Adam's fall. When we call upon a God who hears, expecting His light on our situation, He will hear our call and answer. He will show us the path of life, of light.

He will lead if we are willing to follow. He will empower us to take responsibility for our lives and depend on Him instead of blaming our spouse for our impotence. Even though we've neglected it, He will show us that we have had and do have power. Even if we have stayed in a bad situation out of fear, confusion, lack of faith, trust in a mighty God, or maybe just because it was familiar, we can start exercising our power right now. It's never too late.

The temptation will be to put the blame solely on our abuser and forget that we have work to do for ourselves. We have an unhealthy view of ourselves and the world when we have suffered under extreme abuse.

I encourage you to start exploring the path of forgiveness for yourself as much as for the abuser. I do not mean to stay in an abusive situation. I'm referring to forgiveness that eliminates bitterness and hatred from your heart. You can forgive at a distance.

Be prepared to grieve all that you had wanted and hoped your life would be. For me, I had to mourn a marriage that would last a lifetime, children of my own, and the sadness it caused for my parents as they watched their youngest child's sorrow.

I've had to grieve the "what ifs." I've had to mourn that my husband took advantage of my naivete. I've had to lament the innocence that left me ripe for manipulation and control. I've grieved the years I spent alone, the years I blamed myself, what I didn't get, and the life I didn't have.

Just as with mourning the loss of a person, grieving what you can't have can be extremely painful. There is no way around it. Shoving it down may look like you're fine on the surface, but your grief always finds outlets, and rarely are these outlets healthy.

Once I allowed myself to mourn my childish fantasy of "happily ever after" and grieve what life could have been like, I turned a corner in my healing process. By letting go, I could tell that memory of my younger self that all those feelings of rejection and loneliness were valid. It was OK to be sad about what my first husband robbed me of. It had been a normal response to be devastated after being kicked out of the master bedroom. That young woman who desperately just wanted her husband to love her – her unhappiness was justified.

My youth was wasted on a man who didn't love me and probably couldn't love me. My 25-year-old self didn't have the eyes to see. I missed the red flags, and later, I ignored those I did see because I thought I was stuck and didn't have a justification to leave. What good could come of another argument? I was married for life. There was no way out. I had made a huge mistake, and I had only myself to blame.

But, as God promised in Joel 2:25, "I will compensate you for the years the locusts have eaten."

God has been as faithful to me as He was to the people of Judah when he promised to compensate them for the years the locusts destroyed their crops.

I now have a new marriage that is the opposite of what I had—a night and day difference. We run a business together, and we even go grocery shopping together. He has a wonderful son to whom I've had the honor of being a stepmom. God has provided a dozen amazing women: sisters in Christ, prayer warriors, and trusted confidants. Even beyond the closest few, I now have so many healthy friendships that I have more friends than time to connect with routinely.

My cup indeed overflows!

For all the fruit I didn't produce in the first part of my life, God now uses my story as I talk with women who are going through tough things, things that other women can't understand, but I do. I can step back into those moments of darkness to rest there with them for a moment, then speak truth over them.

I hate what I went through. But now, on the other side, it's almost like watching a movie. I'll never completely forget the pain. I can quickly return to it when a woman shares something with me. I'll tear up and get that twisted, sick feeling in my stomach. I feel her pain because I experienced it, too. There is so much hurt everywhere, but I can be a light in the darkness.

Even while writing this, I did so with tears in my eyes, sometimes to the point where I had to stop and take a moment to collect myself. Other times, I had to allow days between writing to regroup and refocus on my life now.

When trauma has been introduced in our childhood, or we have endured it for years, our body remembers. I'm in my 50s now, and to this day, the mere thought of returning to a particular town makes me sick. A manipulative person trying to bully me leaves me shaking. These deeply engrained responses remain embedded in my nervous system despite my progress.

Healing doesn't mean forgetting or no longer feeling sadness, frustration, or anxiousness. Instead, healing means recognizing, confronting, working through, and finding meaning and purpose. Healing means sorting through those experiences and memories and placing them in a mental suitcase where you can pack and unpack them at will without it being a debilitating experience.

Healing means now when confrontation makes me feel sick, I remind myself I am no longer under Joe's influence. When my hands shake from something that triggers that physiological response, I remind myself that it's just old programming from a threat that no longer exists.

Healing means learning to tap into and control those memories instead of those memories dictating my reactions now. It means never allowing that darkness to stay in the open very long. Healing means those memories serve as a warning to prevent me from repeating the same patterns or choices. Healing means those memories allow me to connect with another survivor of psychological violence. Healing also means not being sorrowful about the first half of my life, it is a reminder of just how desperately I need Jesus.

As Christ followers, we know that all sin grieves a Holy God. That means even those sins we deem small compared to what appears more egregious – like the sin of the one heaping abuse on us. This is why forgiveness is such a vital step in our healing. Forgiving ourselves for staying, leaving, or whatever else we blame ourselves for. It also means forgiving our abuser. Forgiveness does not mean continuing to stay in the path of our abuser. It means forgiving as Jesus forgives us of our sins.

I've talked with enough survivors of abuse to know that when we indeed lay it all at Jesus's feet and when we do what He asks us to do, the shackles of spiritual bondage will be unlocked, and He will meet us right where we are, and He will set us free from Satan's lies.

Jesus will be right there.

He will comfort you.

He will restore your faith.

He will also ask you to examine yourself, your lack of faith, and your weaknesses. He wants what is best for you. He wants you to see what He sees. Trust him.

I pray for each woman reading this book that, just as He has done in my life, you will also experience compensation "for the years the locusts have eaten."

It will not look the way you think it will.

It will be more.

So much more.

CHAPTER 11
STOP THE CYCLE

Maybe, like me, you grew up in the church and, instead of being taught boundaries, were always told to "be nice" and, if someone is mean, just "turn the other cheek."

Perhaps, like me, you were praised for subjugating your wants and needs to keep the peace in your family. A behavior that left you ripe for unhealthy adult relationships. Maybe your childhood was even darker, leaving you vulnerable to even more abuse as an adult.

As I've matured in my faith through Scripture reading, I've come to think that maybe we have been misled. I think it's far too common for Christians to claim it's "God's will" when it's just a way to stay comfortably passive. If we don't speak out, we don't cause waves. If we don't cause waves, our life will be much smoother, won't it? People like amiable people.

It seems all too convenient to our modern sensibilities to do nothing and hide behind phrases that sound like good theology. "If it's God's will, then I'll leave." In talking to women who are in abusive situations, I've heard statements like this because they, like me, have been conditioned into a state of passivity.

Let's look at this response to evil in a way that might be easier to dissect. Suppose you find out a teacher is molesting your child. Would you continue to send your child to that school? If you're thinking, "Of course not!" It's because you can quickly identify that as abject evil being perpetrated on someone you love. You wouldn't ever consider that it's God's will or that the child deserved it because you aren't clouded by guilt; you are seeing clearly out of a basic human adult instinctual response to stop violence against your child.

Why would you think it's God's will that you would be violated? Because you married the guy? Because you should have known better? Perhaps you feel like it's your penance for the sin in your life? I know I certainly thought about all those things! The truth is you're scared. The truth is you don't want to act. That's cowardice in the face of evil; that is not faith.

Whether it's because you don't know what to do, where you'd go, or how you'd leave, or maybe it's because you think you're going to bring condemnation down on yourself for leaving, please hear me: If you are a Christ follower, you are a new creature. God sees you washed clean, as white as snow. Christ already died. Past tense. Done! That means your sins are already forgiven. Atoned for. Past tense. You are not going to disappoint him.

I cannot emphasize this enough. Even if we should go along with the legalistic view of divorce and consider it a sin, well, then, that sin was covered on the cross just like all the others.

> "Therefore, if anyone is in Christ, he is a new creation. The old has passed away; behold, the new has come." (2 Cor 5:17 ESV)

> "And such were some of you [before you believed]. But you were washed [by the atoning sacrifice of

Christ], you were sanctified [set apart for God, and made holy], you were justified [declared free of guilt] in the name of the Lord Jesus Christ and in the [Holy] Spirit of our God [the source of the believer's new life and changed behavior]." (1 Cor 6:11 AMP)

We lie to protect ourselves from whatever our perpetrator accuses us of. We lie to cover up the shame in our marriage. We lie to protect our husbands from social judgment. And we lie to our families. We also gossip, do things we're not supposed to do, and don't do what we're supposed to do. We are doomed without Christ Jesus, no matter what. We can live a perceivable acceptable religious life and *still* be under the weight of our sins. The only thing that brings us salvation is the blood of Jesus. Staying in an abusive marriage will not add to your salvation.

Continuing to live in our private hell here on earth, wallowing in our misery, and allowing ourselves to be violated does not sanctify us. Sanctification comes through spiritual obedience. It is achieved by submitting ourselves, body, mind, and soul to following Jesus. Sanctification does not come from idolizing our spouse or by condemning ourselves.

As you read my story, you may be thinking how awful my story is, seeing parallels in your own life, or thinking, "Lady, you should hear *my* story!" Whatever category you fall into, I hope you are ready to learn you can break free from the spiritual bondage of emotional abuse and heal from psychological violence, all the while knowing God is smiling on you. He isn't judging you. Your old self is dead. He doesn't see it anymore, so why should you?

When we are experiencing psychological violence, we are in a very dangerous cycle. The peril isn't just physical and mental, it is much more severe than either earthly concern. Our enemy is out to destroy us, and he will use other people, other people's sins, our circumstances, and even our own ignorance, weakness, or sense of self-righteousness just as much as he will use our sins to keep us from experiencing the fullness of God. That can have eternal impacts because if the enemy is successful, he can significantly restrict us from leading the life that Christ died for us to enjoy.

Stop being a participant in the drama.

Stop the cycle.

When you stop being the victim, you stop the cycle of abuse. When you disengage, you stop the other person from abusing you. Once you stop being an active party, you will have successfully stopped an entire cycle of abuse in yourself and the other person. You are not powerless; you can stop the cycle.

The one who abuses you may, and likely will, find another victim, but you will have stopped it for yourself. Stopping it will have a ripple effect on those around you. Once we rip anything that isn't God, truth, light, or right thinking out of our lives, we can be more effective conduits for God to work bigger and better things through us. This is not to say we'll be perfect. Of course not. We will never reach perfection until we meet Jesus in eternity.

The life of one who calls themselves a Christian means actively pursuing a life that looks more like Jesus. That quest requires knowing Jesus; we can learn about Him by reading Scripture. There's no reason to be intimidated by Bible reading. I was taught, "Scripture is shallow enough for a child to wade in and deep enough for an elephant to drown in," which is a loose translation of profound words of the theologian and historian, St. Jerome: *"The Scriptures are shallow enough for a babe to come and drink without fear of drowning and deep enough for a theologian to swim in without ever touching the bottom."* I love this so much! We should not be intimidated to start, nor should we ever stop reading it, because there is always more to learn.

We heal and become more like Jesus by reading God's Word and obediently applying it to our lives. Although I already knew Jesus, I was in a state of fear and wallowed in my despair, unable to act. Because I finally faced the truth at age 38, the story of Jesus and the lame man at the healing pool hit home.

> "One who was there had been an invalid for thirty-eight years. When Jesus saw him lying there and learned that he had been in this condition for a long time, he asked him, 'Do you want to get well?' 'Sir,' the invalid replied, "I have no one to help me into the pool when the water is stirred. While I am trying to get in, someone else goes down ahead of me.' Then Jesus said to him, 'Get up! Pick up your mat and walk.' At once the man was cured; he picked up his mat and walked." (John 5:5-8)

This Scripture has so many beautiful layers to it! Did you catch how this is different from the other miracles Jesus performed? Often, Jesus healed because the person knew who Jesus was and they recognized He had the power to heal them. This man didn't even know who Jesus was! When asked the question, the man says he wasn't well because he had no friend to assist him in getting into the healing pool. That sounds like an excuse and the blame game I used to use – a lot. Continue reading through John Chapter 5 to verse 15, and we read that Jesus says to him, "See, you are well again. Stop sinning or something worse may happen to you." In John 9:1, Jesus refutes the idea that one's sin has caused a disease, but in this instance, He tells the man to stop sinning.

I think there are some notable facts to explore about this miracle. First, Jesus gave an instruction: "Get Up." Being an invalid and unable to get into the healing pool means he could not 'get up' on his own accord. This directive was the miracle, for the man could not get up *without* the healing power of Jesus. We cannot obey Jesus on our strength. "Pick up your mat and walk." It was a command not only of action but of forward motion. Here, we see that Jesus told the man to move and to walk. He no longer needed to waste his time in this place, waiting for healing that would never come.

Healing was to be found in the person of Jesus, not in a pool of water. It was a bold directive because it was the Sabbath, and Jews were forbidden from work, even a task as trivial as carrying one's mat. The fact that the man listened to Jesus and did as he was told suggests that he understood the power of who was speaking. Jesus was speaking on the authority of God, not based on a legalistic man-made rule. Jesus did not tell the man to stretch, stay, and then return to what he was doing. His words were, "Get up! Pick up your mat and walk."

Action. Pick up what is yours and leave the place that no longer holds significance or hope for you because you are no longer an invalid. You have been made whole.

As much as I'd love to know more details, the beauty of this story is how it reveals to us that *what* the man did is less important than who Jesus *is*. The man's past is trivial compared to the healing power of Jesus. And for those of us who wait around hoping for someone to help us out of our abusive relationships, for those of us who find perpetual excuses as to why we aren't healthy, the question is:

Do we *want* to be well?

Are we going to turn fully towards Jesus and trust Him? Are we going to get up and take action, trusting that the God who loved us so much that He sent His own Son to the cross to cover our sins sees our pain? Are we willing to allow God to do His work in us?

Are we willing to do our part? We only have to trust, and the most beautiful part is that if we don't have faith, we can pray that the Holy Spirit will fill us with faith!

To be well means not returning to the place. To be well means not to lie back down on our mats. Why bother expending the energy to get out of the first relationship if we're unwilling to do the work to avoid going through it all over again? To extricate ourselves from one abusive relationship only to stagnate under another person's abuse is a sickness.

And yet, so many women do. Over and over.

Read this as if Jesus himself is asking you . . .

"Do *you* want to be well?"

CHAPTER 12
RELIGIOSITY PROBLEM

When people of the Christian faith defend staying in an abusive marriage and other abusive relationships, claiming that it's either God's will for them, it's good to suffer, or because it will bring God glory, I have to wonder, could those all be more lies the enemy uses to destroy us from within?

I think it's important to differentiate between the types of suffering. Suffering for the sake of Christ is altogether different from general suffering. Scripture defines the type of suffering that brings glory to God.

> "Dear friends, do not be surprised at the fiery ordeal that has come on you to test you, as though something strange were happening to you. [13] But rejoice inasmuch as you participate in the sufferings of Christ, so that you may be overjoyed when his glory is revealed. [14] If you are insulted because of the name of Christ, you are blessed, for the Spirit of glory and of God rests on you. [15] If you suffer, it should not be as a murderer or thief or any other kind of criminal, or even as a meddler. [16] However, if you suffer as a Christian, do not be ashamed, but praise God that you bear that name." (1 Pet 4:12-16)

Interestingly, a meddler is "a person who tries to change or have an influence on things that are not his or her responsibility." Could it be our long-suffering years of pretending we can fix our spouse – of being a meddler – is addressed right here in 1 Peter?

In healthy, Godly relationships, it's OK to be the strong one for a while. Your spouse may need and covet your prayers, but when your spouse's behavior hurts you with no accountability and desire to change, all you do is meddle and suffer. There is no ebb and flow, just more meddling and more suffering. The entire time, you're left wondering why you are miserable, lack friends, and why God feels so far away. In these instances, we suffer consequences caused by our behaviors. That should not be confused with suffering because we stand firmly in our faith.

Suffering because we made a bad decision or followed someone else who made a lousy decision also has consequences. Suffering can happen because of proximity to sinful behavior or poor or foolish decisions. Sometimes, we suffer because of our fear or attachment to a human being, a circumstance, or even a desire to keep up an appearance. This type of suffering does not hold the same promise of blessing from God.

Other times, we suffer because we fail to act, confront, and remain afraid of the perpetrator. Suffering for our faith is the opposite. That is when we do take a stand and suffer earthly consequences from a hostile culture. It's critical to distinguish between these things.

God can redeem all suffering and indeed does redeem it when we surrender. I highlight the differences in the types of suffering not to indicate God can't redeem your suffering if you decide to stay in a bad situation, but rather as a counterpoint to the selective use of Scripture that has been used to keep victims from fleeing their abusers and keep women in dangerous environments.

If you're a Christian, you probably already see that anytime something is considered popular or even accepted by our culture, we should proceed with caution because it often means it goes against Scripture. I maintain this also applies to norms within the church. Not everything done or said by "religion" is supported by The Bible. Churches are full of "religiosity," where the emphasis is placed on the appearance of being a Christian rather than cultivating an ever-growing relationship with Jesus.

If you are not a Christian, then you likely have seen things in the church that confuse you or that make no moral sense, such as a church not "allowing" divorce while remaining complicit in pedophilia. No one who truly knows Jesus can adhere to such a vile conviction. You will not find any Scripture reference that supports molesting children or protecting those who do. If you are on the outside, you may see this hypocrisy even more clearly because those inside the church often have a knee-jerk reaction to defend the faith and unquestioningly adhere to whatever they grew up believing.

Our contemporary church heavily relies on passivity as an alternative to facing down evil. To avoid the discomfort of criticism or the consequences of social or political fallout, churchgoers today hide behind things like "I can't judge it; that's for God to judge." Equally thrown about are phrases such as "God's will," or some claim they're "turning the other cheek." Meanwhile, evil not only exists, but it has also taken over our culture and swallowed up our youth.

The story of Jonah is a powerful reminder of what can happen when we run from God and fail to do what he asks us to do.

> "The word of the LORD came to Jonah son of Amittai: "Go to the great city of Nineveh and preach against it, because its wickedness has come up before me."

But Jonah ran away from the LORD and headed for Tarshish. He went down to Joppa, where he found a ship bound for that port. After paying the fare, he went aboard and sailed for Tarshish to flee from the LORD.

Then the LORD sent a great wind on the sea, and such a violent storm arose that the ship threatened to break up. All the sailors were afraid and each cried out to his own god. And they threw the cargo into the sea to lighten the ship.

But Jonah had gone below deck, where he lay down and fell into a deep sleep. The captain went to him and said, "How can you sleep? Get up and call on your god! Maybe he will take notice of us so that we will not perish."

Then the sailors said to each other, "Come, let us cast lots to find out who is responsible for this calamity." They cast lots and the lot fell on Jonah. So they asked him, "Tell us, who is responsible for making all this trouble for us? What kind of work do you do? Where do you come from? What is your country? From what people are you?"

He answered, "I am a Hebrew and I worship the LORD, the God of heaven, who made the sea and the dry land."

This terrified them and they asked, "What have you done?" (They knew he was running away from the LORD, because he had already told them so.)

The sea was getting rougher and rougher. So they asked him, "What should we do to you to make the sea calm down for us?" "Pick me up and throw me into the sea," he replied, "and it will become calm. I know that it is my fault that this great storm has come upon you."

Instead, the men did their best to row back to land. But they could not, for the sea grew even wilder than before. Then they cried out to the LORD, "Please, LORD, do not let us die for taking this man's life. Do not hold us accountable for killing an innocent man, for you, LORD, have done as you pleased." Then they took Jonah and threw him overboard, and the raging sea grew calm. At this the men greatly feared the LORD, and they offered a sacrifice to the LORD and made vows to him.

Now the LORD provided a huge fish to swallow Jonah, and Jonah was in the belly of the fish three days and three nights". (Jonah 1:1-17)

Maybe that's what we're experiencing today: the consequences of generations of men routinely running away from God and away from conflict, causing storms for all of us.

David didn't walk away from Goliath; he faced him. Joshua did not walk away from the battle; he marched his men day after day. After all that marching, he still had to fight a bloody battle. When the people turned the temple into a market, Jesus actively drove them out. He did not say, "My father will judge them harshly," or "Well, it's none of my business," or "Now, everybody, just calm down." Instead, Jesus took swift action.

> "When it was almost time for the Jewish Passover, Jesus went up to Jerusalem. In the temple courts he found people selling cattle, sheep and doves, and others sitting at tables exchanging money. So he made a whip out of cords, and drove all from the temple courts, both sheep and cattle; he scattered the coins of the money changers and overturned their

tables. To those who sold doves he said, "Get these out of here! Stop turning my Father's house into a market!" (John 2:13-16)

Exclamation marks are used in this verse, which means he wasn't passive. Jesus took immediate and direct action. And here is where I sigh, realizing He still didn't sin even in that situation. Even in righteous anger, defending a Holy God, He remained sinless. My heart aches for that kind of healthy response to the sin around me.

That is our role model. He had an appropriate response and carried it out. He did not bemoan their bad deeds, He didn't gossip about it, He didn't make it worse than or better than it was. He saw the problem, and He addressed it.

If we study and reflect on this story more, we might better understand how to respond when confronted with sinful behavior. We don't live in the dark ages where only clergy had Bibles. We don't have to blindly accept what we're told. It is no excuse to claim "because my pastor said so." We can access numerous translations and Bible commentaries at our fingertips for free. We need to learn what God has to say for ourselves. Eternity depends on it.

Let's delve into the three popular lies I've encountered in trying to rectify my faith in the face of abusive situations and learn how to replace those lies with truth.

Lie #1

Let's start with the lie I used myself. It goes a little like this, "If it's God's will, my husband will stop drinking."

The logic here is the same as if we sit at home and watch television while saying, "I'll get a job if it's God's will," without effort. Any thinking person, religious or otherwise, understands that getting hired means taking some type of action like writing a resume, filling out an application, or networking. These are the laws of our world.

If we are in an abusive situation, then why do we sit around and cry that it must be God's will while we do nothing to remove ourselves from the situation? Do we also burn ourselves on the stove and then go back and place our hand back on the stove? Well, some of us do routinely run these sick patterns, and that's exactly what I did for far too long.

The enemy does a phenomenal job of tricking Christians into passivity and complacency under the guise of "God's will." I'm not a therapist, but when I hear the "God's will" statement for staying in an abusive relationship, I can see the individual is either too scared to leave or paralyzed due to trauma. The "God's will" language allows us to continue what we're doing; it soothes us and makes us feel OK about staying in such a miserable state. It fools us into remaining passive and comfortable, even in our discomfort. We'd rather endure the miserable existence we know instead of venturing out into the unknown. I don't know how that gets ingrained in us, but it does.

How could I be terrified of saying and doing the wrong thing for so long and still fear something else? How could I have possibly thought anything else could be worse? Now that I'm on the other side, I am convinced that it is part of the brokenness of our mind and the sickness, which is why we stay. Our minds are so twisted in our present terror that we can't even imagine a world free of it. Once we can imagine a world without turmoil, leaving is bearable, but not until then.

Lie #2

The second lie is more insidious because the Bible teaches that suffering draws us closer to Him. However, as I mentioned earlier, the Bible also outlines different types of suffering. There is a difference between the suffering we bring to ourselves due to sin, the suffering that is part of living in a broken world and suffering for our faith.

> "Therefore, since we have been justified through faith, we have peace with God through our Lord Jesus Christ, through whom we have gained access by faith into this grace in which we now stand. And we boast in the hope of the glory of God. Not only so, but we also glory in our sufferings, because we know that suffering produces perseverance; perseverance, character; and character, hope. And hope does not put us to shame, because God's love has been poured out into our hearts through the Holy Spirit, who has been given to us." (Rom 5:1-5)

This is not a license to continue drinking ourselves into oblivion because it will build our character. You would probably agree that premise is stupid. Of course, being in a state of drunkenness will not build our character. All sinful behavior keeps us from being like Jesus. Therefore, we cannot equate willful sinful behavior with "suffering."

When we're in an abusive relationship where we're lying to cover up for our husband's behavior, when we're not living in truth, when we're not being obedient, not serving, and not doing all the things we should be doing – our suffering is our own doing. We must recognize this crucial difference.

Lie #3

The third lie I've heard women use is that they think their martyrdom will bring God glory. The problem with that is we aren't being martyred for our faith, we're martyring ourselves for someone who is living in a state of sin and a state of violence against us. That isn't martyrdom, that's sickness.

Our churches are often too friendly with our culture, trying to "blend in with" rather than "stand against" it. I want to challenge us to use spiritual wisdom and discernment and examine what the Bible teaches us about God, our roles as Christ's followers, and the marriage covenant.

This is not only because of my struggle of living in a highly abusive marriage but also the number of stories I've heard from fellow Christians who have been shamed and otherwise unsupported by other church members and clergy. I would like us to start looking at the established "rules" accepted as societal expectations in the church and put those against the test of Scripture. I want us to acknowledge that, just like the Pharisees, there are church leaders who are more interested in upholding the church's rules than truly loving the people in them.

The Pharisees of today aren't criticizing the Messiah. Today, they allow their legalism to get in the way of day-to-day shepherding, such as counseling their congregants. Granted, our clergy are typically not trained in counseling. Pastors are not psychiatrists or psychologists. And although many pastors and lay leaders are gifted with the ability to listen and provide godly counsel, it's critical to accept that just as many are not.

It's easy to forget the Pharisees were caught up in their feeling of righteousness because of rule-following so much that their eyes were blinded to who Jesus was. Blinded by self-love and self-adulation, they failed to see Jesus. When Jesus performed actual miracles that defied all logic and all science, they were so indignant that He was breaking a rule that they missed the miracle. Their self-righteousness kept them from seeing that Jesus loved people and glorified an almighty God.

This still happens today. These are the stories I've heard, and they break my heart.

We have church members who hear about a hurting situation or are the ear that hears the pain of a fellow Christian, but they won't extend grace. They find it easier to judge the situation and instead of going into the emotional depths with that brother or sister, they rely on their feelings of piousness and hide behind a couple of verses that support their notion of the world. Instead of listening and getting involved in understanding the pain of a person who is deeply suffering in an abusive situation, they keep their distance, offer platitudes, and pat themselves on the back for quoting Scripture.

Even Satan himself knows and quotes The Bible. Our ultimate enemy didn't hesitate to quote Scripture to tempt Jesus in the desert. This alone is enough to demand reflection.

> "Then Jesus was led by the Spirit into the wilderness to be tempted by the devil. After fasting forty days and forty nights, he was hungry. The tempter came to him and said, "If you are the Son of God, tell these stones to become bread."
>
> Jesus answered, "It is written: 'Man shall not live on bread alone, but on every word that comes from the mouth of God.'"
>
> Then the devil took him to the holy city and had him stand on the highest point of the temple. "If you are the Son of God," he said, "throw yourself down. For it is written:

> "'He will command his angels concerning you, and they will lift you up in their hands, so that you will not strike your foot against a stone.'" Jesus answered him, "It is also written: 'Do not put the Lord your God to the test.'"
>
> Again, the devil took him to a very high mountain and showed him all the kingdoms of the world and their splendor. "All this I will give you," he said, "if you will bow down and worship me."
>
> Jesus said to him, "Away from me, Satan! For it is written: 'Worship the Lord your God, and serve him only.'"
>
> Then the devil left him, and angels came and attended him." (Matt 4:1-11)

How brazen is it to use someone's own words and twist them to mean something other than what was intended? We would say only a narcissist, a master manipulator, or a sociopath would be capable of such things. These characteristics are the embodiment of Satan.

Do you think the enemy is any less savvy when working on us? Of course he uses God's word to manipulate the undiscerning Christian! On top of that, Christians then become his mouthpiece, reigning down unloving words to those who are deep in suffering.

We live in a fallen world, which means we are exposed to negative influences because we live in a very broken world. We are surrounded by those who are influenced by evil, and we also know there is a very real spiritual warfare happening all around us. It is imperative to be vigilant against the enemy's wiles and equally as critical to know Scripture intimately to know what is and isn't from God.

We *do* have victory over our sins. When we choose to yield, we can control our thoughts and actions by the power of the Holy Spirit. But we still fall, every single one of us, every single day.

I'm not here to beat up or to overly criticize the church. What I am trying to do is raise the consciousness of a widespread problem that I have found systematically fails our Christian sisters (and brothers). It is a problem I have lived through, and I feel an obligation to reach out to those still in the throes of navigating an abusive "Christian" relationship because it tears at our very souls and deeply affects our spiritual lives.

I don't want to discourage you from quoting Scripture or supporting a hurting person. I am challenging you to take a moment and pause and prayerfully seek God's word when you are in the position to counsel another person. I hope you do so in the spirit of loving that person first, as you would want to be loved if the situation were reversed. Don't use it as an opportunity to point out every flaw and sin in their life or somehow placate them with meaningless words to make yourself feel better and more spiritual.

I know I'm not alone in having experienced the ugliness of modern-day Pharisees as they smugly assume the position of complete authority, condemning those of us whose marriages did not survive. They do not offer love and acceptance. They stand in judgment on a subject they know nothing about, specifically the trauma and ensuing damage of an abusive marriage.

We can easily cast judgment on the Biblical Pharisees because Jesus directly called them out. We identify their behavior as wrong because we read about their religiosity and categorize it as a past event, as a part of history, and something we would never, ever do. It's easy to forget "there is nothing new under the sun" (Ecclesiastes 1:9). It's easy to forget we have those people living in our midst today.

Jesus makes it clear that those who claim to love God while still actively hating people can't have it both ways. Paul makes it clear that these two cannot coincide.

> "Whoever claims to love God yet hates a brother or sister is a liar. For whoever does not love their brother and sister, whom they have seen, cannot love God, whom they have not seen." (1 John 4:20)

> "Love the Lord your God with all your heart and with all your soul and with all your mind.' This is the first and greatest commandment. And the second is like it: 'Love your neighbor as yourself.' All the Law and the Prophets hang on these two commandments." (Matt 22:37-40)

The church is full of those who purport to be an authority on marriage without ever seeing that an abusive marriage is not a marriage at all. We have contemporary Pharisees who offer trite answers to very heavy, dark, and complex situations, which only heap more abuse onto the person seeking help. I don't have to tell you what the Pharisees did to Jesus.

It should be no surprise that people today say hurtful, unbiblical things to fellow believers, but it grieves me deeply when I hear about it. I've heard of pastors and counselors who were guilty of telling women in evil situations to remain in that environment.

But God tells us to flee from evil. To metaphorically pluck out our eye if it causes us to sin. Twice in the book of Matthew, we are warned:

> "If your right eye causes you to stumble, gouge it out and throw it away. It is better for you to lose one part of your body than for your whole body to be thrown into hell." (Matt 5:29)

> "And if your eye causes you to stumble, gouge it out and throw it away. It is better for you to enter life with one eye than to have two eyes and be thrown into the fire of hell." (Matt 18:9)

> "Do not enter the path of the wicked, and do not walk in the way of the evil. Avoid it; do not go on it; turn away from it and pass on." (Pro 4:14-15)

Truth and freedom are major themes throughout both the Old and New Testaments. We cannot have freedom without truth. If we aren't living in truth, we aren't really free.

What better way to strangle out the truth than to shackle it with lies by those on the inside? Think of your favorite spy or mob movie. The undoing of an organization is completed by a mole a— very convincing and outwardly authentic group member. He pretends and acts like the others but has a serious agenda of exposing or undermining the group. The reason he's successful is that he *is* so convincing.

Yet, we beat ourselves up when we're caught off guard, thwarted, or lied to by the biggest mole of all – Satan. We know the enemy is smart. He roams the earth, seeking to devour us.

Being martyred for our faith is the ultimate testament to what we hold sacred. On the contrary, being a martyr for the sake of being a martyr means allowing oneself to be killed physically or spiritually out of an unwillingness to stand up against what is wrong. That is not saintly; it is weakness in spirit and a sickness of the soul.

I'm not sure how, but it was ingrained in me early on that all sacrifice brought God glory. Even if the sacrifice meant a degradation of my being. It was a deeply rooted sense that it was perfectly acceptable and even noble to allow myself to be treated poorly.

I didn't even know what a "boundary" was until my late 30s, so I thought I was being "good" when people talked down to me, screamed at me, manipulated me, lied to me, and treated me as "less than." For all the sermons, Sunday School, and Lutheran Catechism I attended, I never once learned about God-honoring boundaries. I suppose part of this is due to boundaries being a newer concept. Perhaps as our civilization has deteriorated, we need new words and understandings to interpret our fallen world.

Or, maybe, as our world falls into even more depravity, God himself opens new levels of comprehension and provides new revelations to his Word so that we can still thrive and prevail even as Satan's influence on our earthly world becomes more prevalent and pervasive.

When we're used to living in and around such negativity and listening to the legalism in the Church, it's easy to forget Jesus already paid the penalty for our sins. We fail to remember that we've already been made right with God by the blood of Jesus. Instead, we venture down the same path as Martin Luther, who attempted to atone for his sin by flogging himself. Living under constant abuse is the same thing.

If we convince ourselves that we're doing the right thing by taking the abuse day after day, we can live in just enough peace to get by. If we can believe the lie that the abuse will bring God glory, we can avoid the confrontation of standing up for ourselves or the pain of leaving. For me, I also had a weird sense of self-righteousness and smugness that I could endure. (I told you it was a sickness!) It's the 21st-century version of self-flagellation.

We can't do anything to add to our salvation. Only Jesus' martyrdom was required to overcome evil. We don't add to that salvation by suffering needlessly.

When Jesus talked about plucking out one's eye, it was hyperbole, but it provided a vivid example of how we should do everything we can to distance ourselves from sin and the temptation to sin.

There is no instance where Jesus flogged himself. He was flogged before he was crucified, but that is something he endured at the hands of other people. Jesus did not injure himself.

If we call ourselves Christians, we believe the Bible to be true, and we believe in the indwelling of the Holy Spirit, then we should treat our body as a temple and respect and care for it.

> "Do you not know that your bodies are temples of the Holy Spirit, who is in you, whom you have received from God? You are not your own; you were bought at a price. Therefore honor God with your bodies." (1 Cor 6:19-20)

As Christians, we have the very presence of God dwelling in us. This is why sexual sin is a treacherous sin that our culture has too easily dismissed. If we have the indwelling of the Holy Spirit, what we do to our bodies or allow to be done to us is an affront to a Holy God.

Just as most of us would agree we would not beat ourselves physically, why, then, do we still find it acceptable to beat ourselves up mentally or to be beaten up? Why do we continue to stay in volatile, violent, and abusive situations?

> "May God himself, the God of peace, sanctify you through and through. May your whole spirit, soul and body be kept blameless at the coming of our Lord Jesus Christ." (1 Thess 5:23)

Beating ourselves up mentally is no different than physically torturing ourselves. All too often, mental self-flagellation is nothing more than a way for us to justify our wallowing in self-induced, and dare I say it, self-indulgent pity parties.

Giving up a productive and healthy life to be beaten on by a spouse, mentally or physically, is not supported by Scripture. Sacrificing all the potential good we can accomplish in this life seems to be a ploy of the enemy to keep us shackled from all the good we can do and the fruit we can produce.

> "You did not choose me, but I chose you and appointed you so that you might go and bear fruit—fruit that will last—and so that whatever you ask in my name the Father will give you." (John 15:16)

One step further, if staying in an abusive situation keeps us from growing in our relationship with our Lord, then it is imperative that we abandon this notion of self-righteousness and martyrdom. Staying in spiritual bondage can have eternal consequences. If you're living in a state like I was, you are in danger of missing out on blessings and the joy of an ever-deepening relationship with Jesus.

Jesus overturned the table in the temple when they were blaspheming in his Father's house. If those who were guilty of defiling the church were worthy of having their tables turned over in Jesus' righteous anger, don't we, as his children, have the authority to turn over the proverbial tables when there is a blatant bastardization of the holy sacrament of marriage? When one party is flagrantly fleeing from the marriage commitment and stubbornly refuses repentance, self-reflection, compassion for their marriage partner, or getting help, shouldn't we, in righteous anger, run to assist the one being sinned against?

If a church pastor were to yell, belittle, and demean the members of his church, would we not all agree that something was horribly wrong? Would we stay and take the abuse, citing that it glorifies God? Would we say, "Oh well, I made a commitment to be a member of this congregation, so I guess I have to stay!" Of course not! Instead, we would point out that this pastor was not submitting himself to God but was completely out of order. We would be indignant that one who claims to represent God should be allowed to perpetrate such awful behavior. We would call that blasphemous. We would call it an egregious act against the Holy Spirit.

Wouldn't we?

We would leave or seek to have that pastor removed. Either way, we would not accept it as something we should endure. A pastor is supposed to shepherd his congregation and be a spiritual leader. We know this. We collectively understand and accept this.

Scripture tells us marriage is an analogy of what the relationship between Christ and His church is supposed to look like. Why do we not look at the spouse and say the same thing? Should we not be firmly stating that continuous, unrepentant, abusive behavior is unacceptable? Shouldn't we agree that abuse is not to be tolerated?

Why do so many in the church cling to legalism about divorce instead of acknowledging that any kind of chronic abuse is an outright abomination of the marriage covenant?

Biblical marriage, by definition, is the joining of two people ordained by God. Two becoming one flesh. When the one abdicates his or her role, that leaves one. It doesn't matter that they may still share a home. Two roommates aren't considered married because they live under the same roof. A marriage isn't just a pinky-swear promise, it's a covenant contract (and a legal one) made by two people to love, cherish, and support each other. God even outlines how men are to behave towards their wives.

> "Husbands, in the same way be considerate as you live with your wives, and treat them with respect as the weaker partner and as heirs with you of the gracious gift of life, so that nothing will hinder your prayers." (1 Peter 3:7)

We don't hear this taught. Re-read that verse. This tells men how they treat their wives affects their relationship with their Lord. If that does not state it clearly enough for us, how about this:

> "But if someone does not provide for his own, especially his own family, he has denied the faith and is worse than an unbeliever." (1 Tim 5:8)

Let's go back to the church analogy. If a church of 500 ceased meeting to praise and encourage each other because they fell away into worldly matters, would we continue to call it a church? If the establishment of a "church" is so paramount, why is it no longer referred to as a "church" if members disband? Is it based on the lack of meetings? Is it the lack of structure?

What if one person craved the past and desired corporate worship, and they begged and cajoled those who used to attend? This person prayed for their church revival only to be met with disinterest, cold shoulders, and utter disgust. Say that this goes on for years. Meanwhile, this individual is all alone, without fellowship, without communion. They have no one coming alongside them in times of trial, no pastor to teach them. Would we not call that spiritually stuck? Would we not even call them irresponsible for not finding a place where God was present and working and where they could continue to be fed?

Of course, we would.

This is not a parable in the Bible, so we can't point to a specific story to reference, but we do see where Jesus addresses interactions with unbelievers. He might say to dust the sand off their sandals and find a new church home. He might direct that one person to a thriving church where that person's gifts can be used powerfully—the ultimate slap in the face to our enemy.

When one spouse is unrepentant and blatantly defies his or her spiritual duties and obligations to one's spouse, there ceases to be a Biblical marriage. Especially if there is adultery.

If a pastor walks away from his faith, is he still considered a pastor because once upon a time, he attended seminary? If a church disbands, are they still considered a church?

Why, then, is marriage different?

If God uses marriage to show us His relationship to the church, why would He not take the two parties' participation and heart condition seriously?

God has standards for himself. Don't love Him? Reject his son? It may break His heart, but He will allow that person to spend eternity without Him because He has given us free will.

When Jesus called disciples, His standards were so high that He didn't even allow those fishermen to say goodbye to their families. They had to be all in. So, why do we think God has a smaller view of the sanctity of marriage?

Marriage has been given to us as the most direct look of Christ in relationship to His church. It is meant to be an example to the world. When one's response to emotional abuse in a Christian marriage is that a husband can do what he wants, whenever he wants, with no fear of losing that marriage relationship and the wife must accept it . . . where is the Biblical justification?

The God who turned Lot's wife into a pillar of salt for merely looking back longingly at a sinful, burning city that had been her home? That's a standard.

The Jesus who said it was better to pluck out your eye if it causes you to sin? That's a warning.

The Jesus who forgave but along with it said, "Go and sin no more." That's a command.

Some will point to different passages in Scripture to justify staying in a marriage, and they select scriptures that support submissiveness out of context, for instance.

> "Slaves, in reverent fear of God submit yourselves to your masters, not only to those who are good and considerate, but also to those who are harsh" (1 Pet 2:18)

The trouble with quoting that verse is that the context is how slaves were to relate to their masters. Slaves were in servitude to their masters, not in a marriage union with them. Let us take a look at what the Bible has to say about marriage.

> "Husbands, love your wives, just as Christ loved the church and gave himself up for her to make her holy, cleansing[a] her by the washing with water through the word, and to present her to himself as a radiant church, without stain or wrinkle or any other blemish, but holy and blameless. In this same way, husbands ought to love their wives as their own bodies. He who loves his wife loves himself. After all, no one ever hated their own body, but they feed and care for their body, just as Christ does the church— for we are members of his body. "For this reason a man will leave his father and mother and be united to his wife, and the two will become one flesh." This is a profound mystery—but I am talking about Christ and the church. However, each one of you also must love his wife as he loves

himself, and the wife must respect her husband." (Ephesians 5:25-33)

It makes me glad to be born a woman. All I must do is respect my husband. But men, they have quite a list!

When we are in what is supposed to be a Christian marriage with a spouse who is living with an unrepentant heart and in direct opposition to a God whom they claim to love; when a spouse repeatedly returns to their addiction and abusive behavior, when a husband abdicates his role in the marriage – he has broken the covenant agreement.

God has warned us about these people and against the behavior we even succumb to—not learning from our mistakes.

> "Like a dog that returns to his vomit is a fool who repeats his folly." (Proverbs 26:11)

> "Though you grind a fool in a mortar, grinding them like grain with at pestle, you will not remove their folly from them." (Proverbs 27:22)

We aren't going to change them. *You* aren't going to change him.

Stop going back to your vomit.

Stop being a fool.

I have spent decades trying to rectify this feeling of something not being right in our view of abusive marriages. The more stories I hear of Christian women paralyzed by fear, who have been rendered spiritually and sometimes even physically impotent due to years of abuse, and the more I heal from my own emotional trauma, the more I believe these are all lies by the enemy to keep us in spiritual bondage. It all appears to be a plan of the enemy more than it appears to be the will of God.

Jesus wouldn't coddle abusive behavior. He is not the pale, impotent, soft male portrayed by Hollywood. The man stood up against religious tradition. That alone is evidence of a rare kind of strength.

Many men today can't even stand up to their own children, let alone to an employer or a school board. How many men have the mental strength to take on an entire organization today?

Jesus endured a gory beating with thorns pushed into his flesh and, even after that, carried a cross thought to have weighed 165 pounds for almost half a mile. That's about four bags of water softener salt. How many men can you imagine carrying that much weight for about 10 city blocks in your life? Probably not very many.

Jesus was not a wimp. Jesus was not an enabler. Rather, Jesus was the embodiment of strength. Jesus was the personification of endurance.

Jesus was God . . . here on earth.

Jesus was the model for what men should act like.

Now, let's step back into the context of today's church. The sermons I've heard over the course of my life fall into one of these two categories:

The first is the one I've heard from the Lutheran and Methodist churches that I've attended, which goes something like this: marriage is a covenant, and you must stay at all costs. You only leave if he leaves you first or in the case of adultery. Other than that, you need to pray more, pray harder, and have more faith. When all else fails, just rejoice in your suffering. It puts all the onus on "us" to "do" more. More what? More capitulating? More enabling?

The second sermon type I've heard from my attendance at non-denominational churches is that marriage is a covenant to be honored, and you must make it work. Still, then they add the disclaimer that "if you're in an abusive relationship or don't feel safe, seek help and get out."

It's better, but there's still a problem.

First, the pastor doesn't go into what abuse is or what it looks like. He leaves that alone and focuses solely on staying, praying, and doing. That's all good, but you and I know we do not control the other person. They have free will and will do what they will regardless of how much we pray, cry, beg, or scream at them or God.

Plus, I didn't even know I was being abused. If I didn't understand what abuse was and I took my marriage vows seriously, how could I ever take a pastor's words to mean I had a spiritual way out? I knew I was soul-sick. I knew I cried all the time. I knew things weren't right, but my husband wasn't physically punching me, so in my head, I didn't think I was "abused."

I've never heard any church leader acknowledge how widespread this abuse is. If a pastor has been blessed with a Godly partner and hasn't gone through it, his experiences are relegated to third-party stories and movies – hardly a snapshot of the real world.

Of course, the church should support the restoration and healing of marriages, but that is predicated on both parties wanting to work towards change and healing and towards that restoration. The following passage seems to convey mutual consent:

> "If any woman has a husband who is an unbeliever, and he consents to live with her, she should not divorce him." (1 Cor 7:13)

God does heal us when we confess and repent, but therein lies the rub. What happens when one party refuses to acknowledge their actions, sins, and acts of deception? What happens when one side has no desire to repent? When one party rejects God?

What about then?

Yes, God does soften hearts. And I weep tears of joy when I hear stories about marriage restoration. But let's talk about when we don't get the miracle. Let's talk about when God allows the person to stay right where they are.

Mature Christians know that God does not answer all prayers as we want them answered. We also know that not everyone will experience a heart change. If we can acknowledge those facts, why is the church not addressing these challenges? Why do pastors shy away from these topics? Why aren't churches at large addressing these issues?

When we identify areas where the organized church fails, the body of believers must become the solution we desperately need. The original church was built on community and lay leaders. Let you and me fill the need that our culture won't and our pastors can't.

This is a call to every one of you who has been through abuse to do the work and heal fully so that you can speak life into others. Why not set out to heal so that you can reach out and encourage others? I'm throwing down a challenge to get to a place where you can reach back and be the church to other women in desperate need of healing.

I prayed and I prayed, and I prayed, and I prayed, and I prayed.

I begged, I pleaded.

I went to church. I was a Christ follower all during my first marriage. I had a very robust prayer life even then. I prayed throughout my day - every day. God did not soften my husband's heart. My husband never got sober. My husband never got better. Those prayers were not answered the way I expected they would be.

What, then, church?

Why does the church at the macro level continue to marginalize what I believe is a rampant problem even within our faith communities?

Why are churches silent on some social issues but not others? Is it because some topics are trending in the media? Or is it because they're more pressing culturally? Perhaps the lies are clearer. Or maybe it's just easier.

As Christians, surely, we can do better than tell a woman (or man) to pray more.

We need to start bringing the prevalence of emotional abuse into our cultural discussions. And it must be brought into our church discussions. For those of us who have experienced it, emotional abuse permeates our entire lives. It affects our relationships with everyone outside of the abuser. It affects our work, families, and friendships just as much as our spiritual lives. Left unresolved, it can even sever us from a relationship with Jesus as we ourselves slip into the shame and darkness of complacent behavior.

Not only have I experienced this within my family, but I've also had friends from whom I ultimately walked away. I've had clients I was all too happy to be free of when I noticed their abusive language. It's rampant, and it's everywhere.

So, what should the Christian response be when one is in a day-to-day living hell, and their spouse has refused help, abdicated their spousal role, and rejected them?

In speaking with pastors, I've learned that they are not taught about abusive relationships in seminary. Their training is strictly theological. Pastors are not licensed therapists. Although some pastors have a natural gift in this area, we should not expect it to come with the title.

So where does that leave the heart of the Christian woman who loves Jesus, who desperately wants to live a godly life but finds herself in a marriage that is hurtful and ungodly?

From my experience and working with others like me, I believe that the church does not know *how* to address it -- so it doesn't.

Churches will take a hard stance on homosexuality or abortion. Still, they refuse to do a deep dive into something that is equally as pervasive in our culture and our churches: emotional abuse – or, as I prefer to refer to it – psychological violence.

It doesn't just come from a spouse. It can come from a parent, a sibling, a friend, a co-worker, or a boss. This issue of emotional abuse is everywhere in our culture. It's exacerbated by reality television shows and social media, where dysfunctional and abusive behavior is not only on display but rewarded by viewership. The voyeurs at first find it repulsive. But like a car wreck, they can't stop watching. After a while, it is normalized, laughed at, and celebrated.

If you're reading this book and either know or suspect that you are in an abusive relationship, I hope you will find tools for moving forward. If you are the family member or friend of someone who you know or suspect is in an abusive relationship, please keep loving them, and don't dismiss them along with their abuser – they need you. There are ways you can protect yourself, have clear boundaries, and still love and support that person.

Does God work miracles? Yes.

Does he always? No. Well, not in the way we expect them, anyway.

Regardless of who you are in this scenario, please understand you are not alone.

There are millions, yes, millions just like you.

There is a way forward.

I am proof.

CHAPTER 13
GRIEVE AND GROW

One crucial element to healing is allowing yourself to grieve. I had to allow myself to mourn my entire life of what ifs, and what could have been.

Whether or not you stay in your marriage (or whatever abusive relationship you may find yourself in), you will need to grieve the loss of the relationship, your mistakes, and the life that could have been, along with the relationship you never had. It is a death. It's a death of innocence, a death of hope, and a death of a future you had envisioned or could have had. Allow yourself to grieve that death and mourn those losses.

Grief is healthy as we process the memory and loss of something, but it can become unhealthy when we wallow in it and find excuses to stay in that mental state.

Do you like the attention you receive from friends or family members? Have you found you like it when people offer sympathy or, better yet, start badmouthing your spouse? Watch out. This is a slippery slope. When we become accustomed to neglect, as I was, we can very easily welcome unhealthy attention. Any attention that isn't yelling and belittling feels good. If we aren't careful, we can quite easily become narcissistic moving forward as we explore our new landscape of possibilities, insisting on having our way for a change.

Certainly, you will need to learn what you like and don't like after years and maybe decades of not knowing your preferences. You do need to discover those things before moving into another relationship.

Asserting yourself will be new to you, but don't become so dogmatic that you, in turn, become the person you escaped. Hold yourself to a higher standard to recalibrate without losing yourself while you uncover your new world. Be watchful because you are in a very fragile state, and if you have never created and held to healthy boundaries before, you may not know what they look like in others either.

This is a time to go introspective. Get yourself into counseling. Read everything you can and listen to mental health professionals on podcasts. Do not jump into dating. Throw yourself into new hobbies that allow you to be outside in nature or find ways to serve in your community. Find things to do that you were forbidden to do previously.

The reason we are so lost isn't because of a lack of God's presence or even because we live in a sinful world. It's not Satan's fault. We only need to look in the mirror to see why we don't have answers. We have access to the living word of God, and I'll admit how often I become complacent. I have easily gotten caught up in my self-righteous thoughts and rely on my favorite verses. It's easy to think I have the right answer because I can recite those verses. Meanwhile, there are more than 30,000 verses in the Old and New Testaments. I must remind myself to be humble and curious about the things I don't know. I also, need reminding that God is continually at work in me.

The best defense is a good offense. The best defense we have against those who are under the influence of dark spiritual forces, against our sin and Satan, is the spiritual offense of knowing God's word.

Have you noticed that the only actual weapon in spiritual armor is the Holy Spirit?

> " . . . and the sword of the Spirit, which is the word of God." (Eph 6:17)

It is not a suggestion. It is part of the equation. We do not get to be passive or rest solely on defense. That is not Biblical truth. Putting on the armor includes mostly defensive measures, but that sword of the Spirit is powerful imagery. Yes, the armor will help protect you. Still, none of those elements will strike down evil thoughts, evil advances against you, demonic influences, or Satan himself. Only God's *Word* does that.

Reading and applying God's Word was paramount for me, but I also had to actively pursue change in behaviors and thoughts that had led me into that darkness in the first place. It is like the difference between asking for forgiveness versus true repentance. We can say we are sorry, but the true test of the authenticity of an apology is whether one continues the behavior repeatedly.

When we are looking at healing from abuse, it isn't enough to grieve what's been lost, as that will keep you focused on the negative and the past. You need new thought patterns, beliefs, and behaviors moving forward to be well. It may very well take reevaluating other unhealthy relationships in your life.

Recognizing the depths of manipulation, gaslighting, and emotional abuse takes years to uncover. It doesn't happen all at once. The light switch does not just go on. It's more of a dimmer, slowly, very slowly, growing brighter as more and more is revealed.

As more lies are exposed, the more truth prevails, and the more you will uncover your inherent worth. You are beautiful—not because I say so but because your Creator says so. The One who created everything created you in His image.

> "So God created mankind in his own image, in the image of God he created them; male and female he created them." (Psalm 139:13-14)

If you have asked Jesus into your heart and proclaim Him to be your Lord and Savior, your Father sees you as redeemed, washed clean – as clean as snow. What, my friend, can be more beautiful than that?

When you search for your identity, search for it in the only one who has the power to call something "good," as He calls His creation. You were created in His likeness.

The horrible nightmare you may be living right now is not what God created but a result of a fallen world. It is the result of sin, the unchecked sin of one allowing sin to run rampant in their life and wreak havoc on yours. That is a result of sinful humanity.

The world will tell you there is no hope. Your church or pastor may even turn away from you. I have heard countless stories of women being told things by Christian counselors and pastors that they cannot get a divorce, leaving women feeling as if there is no way out. They are told it is sinful.

So is gossiping.

So is lying.

So is judging others.

So is bitterness.

If all of those sins are forgiven and redeemed, why not divorce? We were all born into sin, and it is only by the saving blood of Christ that we are washed clean and redeemed. Being a new creation should mean that Christians can and should do better in their responses to those in abusive marriages. God no longer counts that sin against us; therefore, we should not hold that against another.

Women will stay in an endless cycle of abuse, bitterness, resentment, and acting out their sinful behavior as a result. This cycle of sin continues day after day, year after year, generation after generation. I am here to suggest that it's time to stop that cycle.

Yes, we must look to Scripture for our answers. And no, the answer is not to conform to the world and its solutions.

Jesus said, if your eye causes you to sin, pluck it out. Although primarily referenced to sinful lusts and desire, Matthew Henry's commentary states, "We must think nothing too dear to part with, for the keeping of a good conscience."

> "And if your eye causes you to stumble, gouge it out and throw it away. It is better for you to enter life with one eye than to have two eyes and be thrown into the fire of hell." (Matt 18:9)

That could mean you will face ostracization from family and disparaging comments from friends for being divorced. It could mean you face the deterioration of your false sense of self that you are a "good" person or a "good" Christian. Instead, we know we are new creatures, which means we are God's righteousness in Christ Jesus, not from any goodness we have earned.

When you fully fling yourself at Jesus' feet, you will find all of that is meaningless anyway. Earthly and man-made constructs will fade away. Living in the fullness of Christ means nothing comes before your praise, adoration, and obedience to your creator.

When Christians leave their marriages, they often do so with a great deal of guilt and condemnation and never find their way back to their Creator's grace. Romans 5:20 reminds us, "Where sin abounds, grace abounds." Listen, there is nothing that can separate you from Christ Jesus.

> "For I am convinced that neither death nor life, neither angels nor demons,[a] neither the present nor the future, nor any powers, [39] neither height nor depth, nor anything else in all creation, will be able to separate us from the love of God that is in Christ Jesus our Lord." (Rom 8:38-39)

If you know Jesus, then leaving abuse is a step in acknowledging Jesus is also Lord of your situation. If you do know Jesus, then when you repent of your participation in the sin cycle, you will find grace and forgiveness.

CHAPTER 14
CHASE JESUS

One level of healing came from reading the Old Testament all the way through. I discovered the treacherous condition of fallen humanity and found hope in the process. In reading, I saw the pattern of the Israelites. They worshiped God and received profound protection and blessings, only to turn away from Him. After suffering the consequences of sin and rebellion, they would repent and turn back toward Him. God would accept their repentance and shower them once again with blessings. Then, they turned away again. They suffered again, but then they would once again repent. God would, once again, bless them. This cycle went on generation after generation after generation after generation.

Each time God's chosen people repented, God forgave and blessed them. I found it comforting to learn that God loves us so much that He never stops loving His children. He also never stops forgiving and bringing us back under His blessings when we repent.

It's a beautiful reminder of just how good our God really is. For me, God's goodness has meant everything. I wouldn't have been able to escape from the desperate situation I was in, nor would I have been able to heal without God's goodness.

> "I will repay you for the years the locusts have eaten – the great locust and the young locust, the other locusts, and the locust swarm – my great army that I sent among you." (Joel 2:25)

Even though the above verse was a promise made to a nation of people, it spoke to me deeply when I read it a few years ago. That's the beauty of God's word. It's the Living Word. It can transcend time and place and speak to our hearts. I have seen God do this for me. He has repaid me for those awful years filled with my own plague of emotional duress. My life is so full now! It is so filled with all that is good in this life – a loving spouse, friendships, and church community. I can't read the words of Joel and think anything but that all of the life devoured by poor choices and enemy attacks has been restored.

God redeems our sins when we repent, turn away from sin, and seek Him with all we've got. I also know nothing happens without Him seeing. Couldn't God have placed one wonderful friend at my church who could've poured truth into me? Couldn't God have prevented me from attending the event where I met Joe? Couldn't God have placed a man in my life who would've cherished me back then? Of course, He could have. But He didn't.

I recently heard that God has a plan for our fruitfulness in this life; therefore, He allows what needs to happen to bring us to that mission. Is that the explanation? Did I suffer to learn the depth of his kindness and mercy and call me into a deeper relationship with Him? If that is why, surely that is enough of a reason. Did I endure that pain to bring light to these issues? If that is true, He will use my story to bring hope and healing to others. Either way, He had me in His grip all along!

It doesn't matter if what you're living in results from sinful choices, bad judgment, or an abject evil presence in your life because God is bigger than any of it!

Even though my life went down a dark path, God pulled me out. God has repaid me for those lost years, but not because He owed me anything. It was out of His ultimate goodness. I clung to Him, chased Him down, and stood against Satan's stronghold, and I believe these blessings now are the harvest for obedience. He has given me years of absolute joy to replace the years of sorrow and pain because He is good and a God of second chances.

There are times when we can read what God did in the past on a macro level and point to how He works similarly in our lives. It doesn't diminish the original story. It doesn't make us the hero. It's just God speaking to us and letting us know He is here. He is still relevant. He cares for us just as He did for those whose lives are documented in Scripture.

For example, I have experienced several partings of the Red Sea events, where just in the nick of time, a resolution came through that could not have been foreseen. This allows me to relate to Biblical events, feel the relief of experiencing God's goodness, and say, "Yes, I understand how that feels!" instead of merely reading something from history and moving on as if it has no relevance today.

I've read the book of Joel in the past with not much thought, but when the time was right, I read those words, and my heart skipped. The words leaped from the page, and that small voice in my head said, "Yes!"

My healing is part of my story.

Healing can become your story.

I don't know how God will work in your life. I can't promise you anything because God isn't formulaic. He isn't transactional in the sense that if you do X, He will do Y. He is relational.

Surrendering to Christ is paramount. It comes before anything else. That surrender, I believe, is the path to healing. However, a spiritual surrender to Christ is very different from saying, "I have to wait and see if my husband drinks today," "I need to allow him to hit rock bottom," or "I can't help my attitude or my situation." Don't mistake surrendering to Christ and His will for passivity against strongholds in your life.

It can be painful to submit fully. Human nature demands to be in control. As women in the 21st century, we have been programmed to believe we can do anything and that we deserve to have it all without compromise. The song by Irving Berlin comes to mind, "Anything you can do, I can do better." We apply that to our boss, men, and sometimes God. Even as new creatures in Christ Jesus, we fall back into old habits and conform to the culture.

Despite how awful it will feel initially, yielding our will to our Creator becomes freeing. He takes the weight off of us, and when we're no longer in a power struggle with Him, the burden of life becomes easier and more peaceful.

I know how exhausting and humiliating it is to face ourselves and the mess of our lives, whether by our own choices or not. But a festering wound must be cleaned. The alcohol used to clean out a wound is excruciating for a few minutes but necessary to get out the gunk. Without that step, healing can't even begin.

And so it goes with digging into the psychological aspects of our lives. Going deep and dealing with all the emotional junk is the only way to cleanse yourself. It's the only way to move forward to complete healing. Giving it all over to the One who loves us more than anyone else ever will – that is a sweet surrender.

In some contexts, a 12-step process can be beneficial. However, in myself and many women I have talked with, the 12-

step process can further paralyze women in crisis because it's part of the same message our abusers have perpetuated.

You change.

You make amends.

You be better.

If you've been on the receiving side of psychological violence, this sounds all too familiar to what we hear day in and day out.

"It's YOUR fault"

"If YOU didn't do ___, I wouldn't have to yell at you."
"If YOU just listened to me . . .

"YOU should be more submissive.

The addict, the alcoholic, the narcissist – they all desire control. They *do* control. That is their nature, so let them do their 12 -steps. I found that the program caters to the addict, to the narcissist. For those of us who have been on the receiving end of those personalities and suffered extreme emotional trauma, I recommend we focus on healing, and there's only one Person who has the power to heal us completely and miraculously.

His name is Jesus.

The best part about Him is you can rest. All you have to do is surrender and allow Him to work in you.

> "Come to Me, all who are weary-laden, and I will give you rest." (Matt11:28)

This book is not to encourage or affirm your divorce. If you can stay, stay. Divorce will cause spiritual, emotional, and financial brokenness and hardship. I can't even wish it on the people I dislike the most – that's how atrocious it was. I was in spiritual bondage. I paid a heavy price to leave because I wanted to be free to chase Jesus.

I was determined to heal, not remain stuck. I desired to help other hurting women. I desperately wanted my experiences to bring some good.

I threw myself into self-reflection and repentance. I chased after Jesus, determined to work on my faith and to know Jesus even more. I desired a life that would glorify God. I wanted to be useful to Him!

I urge you to prayerfully weigh your circumstances. Are there children involved? Are they at greater risk if you stay or leave? The consequences of divorce may be greater than what you will gain. You need to prayerfully consider all aspects of a decision like this. There is only one answer I can give to you that applies to all situations.

The answer is as simple as it is complex.

Chase Jesus.

Every day, in all you do, chase him. Run after him. Do not relent; do not get distracted by the world. Run as if your life depends on it because it does.

I have noticed one thing in my life that is true: whether in our physical being or our emotional world, the stronger you are, the stronger you become. Conversely, the weaker you are, the weaker you become.

Staying in an abusive relationship and relinquishing power to another person is akin to muscle atrophy when we stop exercising. The longer we go without working out, the weaker we become. The longer we stay in an abusive relationship, the more we have normalized it, and the more we will have to fight to extricate ourselves from it.

I wanted out, but years of the "marriage is forever" mindset kept me from exploring my options. Something deep within me dared to whisper something was not right. I experienced years of misery, but in my sickness, in my weakness, I did what was easier. I clung to a false hope that he would change.

As things progressed and I started to awaken to reality, I started allowing myself to take that mental journey of "What ifs." What if I left? What if I could get out? An innate survival instinct was triggered, and the more I entertained the idea, the stronger it grew. And the path was made for me to exit gracefully, without being financially screwed over by him and without being physically harmed.

My story isn't about strokes, being married to an alcoholic, or even abuse. My story is about God's never-ending love. My story is about His grace, His abundance, His extravagant love. He loved me too much to let me stay stuck in a dark place.

He HEARD me!

He created my desire to be closer to Him. When I heard God compelling me to act, I listened and acted. When I began to move, He began to move.

When I fought, He came up beside me with His power and His might and fought for me.

He was the hail as he was on Israel's enemies, as He was for Joshua.

He restored me as He did Job.

People will fail you, but not God.

Ask. Listen. Trust.

Cry out.

Take up arms against the enemy.

Years of living in such a psychologically violent environment kept me shackled to an endless cycle of trying to please people so I could remain in their good graces. I craved love and affection, and if I complied, they would make room in their hearts for me – or so I thought.

The trouble was that I didn't learn any coping tools growing up, and I didn't seek out tools as an adult because I wasn't even aware I needed any. I continued to do what I had always done, which was stay in unhealthy relationships, which in turn kept me from the healthy ones. I drove away decent, well-adjusted people.

At a visceral level, I knew I didn't like how these relationships felt and wanted something different, but it was my reality, and I didn't even know what a healthy relationship looked like. Due to that shortsightedness, I remained in an awful loop of isolation and relationships that caused me pain.

It's similar to being sick for a long time, and when you finally feel better, you realize you almost forgot what it felt like to be healthy. That's how it is with emotional health, too.

It has taken me 13 years to heal. It's been a long process. At times, I would make giant strides forward, and then it would feel like I was backsliding emotionally.

The damaged way of thinking and reacting was such a part of me that it took a solid eight or nine years to fully comprehend it all. It took all of those years to see just how manipulative Joe was. It took almost a decade of healing to realize I couldn't trust anything from that period of my life.

What he told me about friends, coworkers, and stories about his work trips, were they all lies? Partial lies? Had he lied from the time I met him?

I will never know the answers.

What I do know is that he preyed on my naivete and my trusting nature. He manipulated my faith, twisted scripture, and insulted and humiliated me.

And I took it.

Not only did I accept it, I fell into a sick ritual of feeling sorry for him, defending him to others, and trying to help him – never understanding he would never get better.

I didn't understand the depths of his emotional state. I didn't understand back then that I enabled him to play me like an instrument.

Outwardly, I kept a brave front. Oh, did I keep up the show! Inwardly, I was withering away. I was dying to have a true partner and longed for close friendships—two things that eluded me no matter how hard I tried. Healing took me a long time because I truly did not understand just how damaged I was.

I thought once I was out from under his control, I would naturally heal and be OK. But healing comes after removing the source of an infection. We can cover it up, but until the source of the infection is removed, we won't be healed. We need Jesus. We need Jesus so that we don't feel the need to make others happy to feel loved.

We are already loved! Why do we seek acceptance from everyone except Him?

Healing requires looking deep inside and into our past to see where our thoughts and behaviors originate. It requires looking at our lives through a different lens, and once we uncover the truth, we can delve into things we would rather avoid.

The phrase "eyes wide shut" describes how I lived the first half of my life, believing my world was good, right, healthy, and normal.

I believed I was healthy. Oh, the mockery that must've made of me! The people who interacted with me – what must they have thought?! I was so broken. My overreactions! My emotions! I was incapable of healthy friendships because I was not a healthy person. It has only been through introspection and willingness to change that I have finally been able to break free of the hold that abuse had on me.

I can finally see clearly. I finally stopped the cycle. I finally feel as if I'm healed. God has restored all that I was robbed of.

He gave me:

A loving marriage.

A better stepson than I could ever have imagined.

A vibrant church where my new husband and I serve together.

And friends. I have so many dear, cherished friends. Not just two or three, but I have more than 12 women in my life who I can call and share without judgment. These are women I pray for and who will pray for me. These women lift me up and encourage me. Their fantastic humor makes me belly laugh. We laugh together, cry together, pray together, and rejoice together.

My life has been restored.

My new family and my friends are what give me a little bit of heaven right here on earth.

I will likely always struggle with the remnants of emotional scar tissue, as there is always a new situation that I have to reframe or pause to consider an alternative response. That may never go away. But the great news is that those new, healthy responses are increasingly my new default.

With each passing year free of spiritual bondage, the memories dissipate, and they are further and further distanced from my mind and from my nervous system.

I know there will be more seasons of sadness and hardship because that's life. But, for now, I feel God has replaced the years the locusts had eaten up, and He has blessed me with marriage and friendships beyond what I could have ever dreamed to even ask for.

I suppose it's a good thing we can't see what life has in store for us when we're young because who of us would want to press on?

And yet, despite all the ickiness. Through all the darkness and sadness, here I am. I've come through it.

But what is survival alone? What is perseverance alone? Is it only for ourselves? I don't believe it is. I believe that when we are restored, it is meant for a greater purpose. For me, that means showing other women there is hope. To me, being restored means being repaired so that I can be useful.

God can redeem our story. God can get glory out of any situation.

Ask for revelation.

Ask for healing.

Seek him with everything you've got.

He will come to you in all your brokenness and you-ness. And little by little, He will help you up, keep you standing, and heal all those deep, dark things.

He will clean you up. But first, you must desire change. You must want more. You must desire Jesus more than you want anything else in the world.

As much as I would have loved to have lived a life as it could have been, without uninformed choices, without abuse, without sadness, without that incredible darkness –God still provided a way back for me.

Just as after Adam and Eve's fall, God provided Jesus as our way back to Him by putting our sins on Jesus and washing us clean so that we could walk with Him in fullness in a personal relationship, as He did with Adam and Eve. He knew the path my life would take and provided a way back to a deeper relationship with Him—a second chance at marriage, a second chance at a family.

He placed me in front of a man who needed what I had and who had what I needed.

God healed my heart of the past hurts, old wounds, and all that trauma.

Your restoration will be different than mine.

The one thing that will be the same is restoring the right relationship with your heavenly Father.

Chase Jesus and you will find Him.

Chase Jesus and He will heal your wounds.

Chase Jesus because nothing else really matters.

CHAPTER 15
ACCIDENT WAITING

Why do we have streetlights other than to illuminate the night? Why do we use flashlights other than to cast light into the darkness? Light does not flee from darkness but sharply cuts through and forces a path into the darkness. Even the tiniest amount of light can penetrate the darkest dark.

In the same way, we need to project light into our world and onto our lives so that all will be revealed and we can live in truth. The safest and wisest place to live is "in the light," in God's truth—Biblical truth.

The popular term "my truth" is a slippery slope of wordplay that can easily morph into an alternate reality where truth does not exist. But it can also mean the other part of the story that hasn't been heard.

There are factual truths, and then there is the context that makes up part of the larger story. Sometimes, context can be one's perspective or even feelings. On a superficial level, I think this is what most people mean when they use the phrase "my truth," but as Christians, we need to tread carefully.

I was in a little fender bender right after college. It was early morning on a city street, and I was focusing on the streetlights and the traffic ahead of me, trying to gauge if the light would change. I was also messing with the radio. I was, admittedly, distracted.

Two cars ahead of me, the driver slammed on the brakes to avoid blocking an entrance to a parking lot instead of slowing up to the car in front of them. That overreaction caused the driver in front of me to slam on her brakes. She stopped just shy of the other person's rear bumper. Although I, too, slammed on my brakes the instant I saw it happen, I was just a little too close and on a downward slope, so I ran into the car in front of me.

Facts.

Nothing absolves me from that fault. I was the one that caused the car accident. The whole point of keeping a great deal of distance between you and the car ahead of you is to account for someone else's error. I was following too closely to stop at such short notice. Now, the entire context is important and is part of the story. The driver who slammed on their brakes, which caused the whole chain reaction, wasn't driving much better than I was since they weren't watching the traffic pattern and didn't anticipate what their brake stomping would potentially do. It was city traffic. We were all following just a little too closely. The truth is the entire context.

It doesn't matter that another driver made a poor decision. It doesn't excuse my behavior.

But it does show how, when we are not completely focused on what is ahead of us when we are not doing what we know we should be doing, when we are even a little distracted, when we are not accounting for other's errors—and on the topic of this book—accounting for other's sins, we too can get trapped into bad situations by focusing on the wrong things, being distracted, and not protecting what is ours to protect.

I should not have been following that close. Plain and simple.

I should not have married Joe.

I should not have been distracted by my radio. Plain and simple.

I should not have allowed my desire to be with someone to be stronger than my instinctual twinges of bad feelings.

I should have kept a proper distance between me and the car in front.

I should have been in a Bible Study with other women and reading my Bible daily.

I was distracted, focused on the wrong things, and allowed my loneliness and desire to be married to override my good sense.

All truths. All facts. All a part of the context of how I ended up making such a mess of my early life.

The fact my ex-husband had his slew of problems was also true. It doesn't absolve me from my stupid decisions – I completely own my naiveté and lack of good judgment, but it is also part of the story. Another person could be as naïve, and her marriage could be just fine. Some things happen we cannot explain. But, when we are not focused on where we should be, things happen to us because we are not equipped, or we choose not to see the warning signs when others' behavior goes awry.

In the example of that car accident, I should not have glanced down and should have allowed more space. It all would have been avoided if I had been alert and had given my full attention to the traffic ahead instead of just the car in front of me. The other person's actions would still have occurred, but the ensuing fender bender would have been avoided.

Had I been focused on growing spiritually, on ways to get more involved in my community, where God was leading me, and not on my being alone, perhaps I would have had the discernment to reject the idea of marrying a man who was not a suitable mate.

Here's the thing: I was trying to get my career together. I was busy working three jobs to pay rent and being a responsible adult. I was active in a local church and worked with their youth group. I had sought out several single groups at different churches. I was trying to make friends! It wasn't as if I had rejected God or was completely self-absorbed, but looking back, I wasn't completely focused on where I needed to be.

I was distracted. I was living out some blueprint passed down to me that said the only way to be happy was to be married. From my childhood, I had developed self-sabotaging thoughts of not being enough, not being wanted, and that something external was the only answer to that gaping hollowness I felt.

Without women around me pouring in good things, without close friends offering Godly perspectives, I drowned in my loneliness, and the next thing I knew, I was married to someone who belittled me, humiliated me, raged at me, lied to me, and gaslighted me – for 13 and a half, very long years. Ironically, it exacerbated my loneliness to a catastrophic level.

When we are isolated, the enemy can distract us. We may feel like we're on the right path. Remember, it wasn't like I wasn't watching where I was going that day of the accident, I was only momentarily distracted. A split second of distraction and BAM I ran into the car in front of me. A *second* is all it took.

RESTORING THE YEARS THE LOCUSTS HAVE EATEN

This is where we all go wrong.

Distractions.

Busyness.

Fear.

Lack of community.

All things our enemy loves.

CHAPTER 16
GUIDE TO HEALING

"Do you want to get well?" (John 5:6) Just as Jesus asked the invalid man who had been in his condition for 38 years if he wanted to get well, he's asking you the same thing. Do *you* want to get well? If you do, get up and walk! It is in the belief that you can that you will.

Healing won't just happen. I've known too many people who have just moved on to the next relationship, wrongly thinking the problem was all the other person. After the subsequent courtship, they find themselves again in a bad relationship. History will repeat itself. You will again be mistreated if you haven't healed the past hurts.

Change requires work—a lot of hard work. Ask yourself if you are willing to take the necessary steps to heal to make the pain of leaving worthwhile.

If you choose to divorce, you will have a lot of healing to do. It won't be easy, and it will not happen in just a year or two. Healing is a process. If you choose to stay in your marriage, you are going to need every bit of support you can gather. Regardless of your path, you need this chapter.

If you stay in your marriage, these areas of focus may just help you find a happy coexistence with your spouse that you never thought possible. If you leave and desire a godly marriage the next time around, you have serious work to do so that you can enter into a marriage with as little emotional baggage as possible.

These are the things that helped me grow spiritually and firmly root my identity in Christ. They are how I healed and was able to move into marriage with someone who cherishes me. It was through this process that I was able to develop deeply meaningful friendships. Doing the work is how I could assign purpose and meaning to all that I had suffered and move forward.

I've outlined six things that will grow your faith and facilitate your healing:

- Bible Study
- Praying
- Community
- Serving
- Forgiving
- Christian Counseling

I. Active Bible Study: Use a Study Bible.

If you do not own a study Bible, buy one. It is a worthwhile investment that will enrich your life. God can speak to you without one, but when we don't understand something, we tend to gloss over it and move on instead of digging in deeper. Without studying context, we also run the risk of misunderstanding and misquoting scripture, just as we've addressed previously with those who fail to minister to hurting abuse victims. When we don't know what scripture says, it leaves us vulnerable to those who misuse it to shame us or to lead us astray.

Some verses and chapters can be difficult to understand. A study Bible will help you with context and provide additional scriptures supporting the same idea. It will also aid you in your spiritual growth.

If you want to delve deeper, I highly recommend Matthew Henry's Commentary. There are two types of people: those who love books and those who don't. If you don't like books, you can simply Google "Matthew Henry's commentary" and include the chapter and verse you're searching for, and you'll find what you're looking for. If you love books, buy the hard copy; it's a gloriously thick book. Rather than be intimidated by it, I find it a wonderful reminder of how deep God's word is and proves just by the sheer volume of pages that we should never think we know all there is to know about God's word.

We wouldn't read quotes from any other book and claim to have read it, so why do we do it with the most sacred book? It is not Bible quote reading; it's called Bible "Study." That means committing our time and attention to gaining knowledge. Reading a quick quote can be a great way to keep God's word in front of us, and He'll use that to encourage you or for you to encourage someone else on given days, but don't confuse that with studying the Bible.

Work on the habit and discipline of devoting time to reading, contemplating, and applying His word.

> "Man shall not live by bread alone, but on every word that comes from the mouth of God." (Matt 4:4)

Select a time of day to commit to reading and studying scripture. Schedule it in your calendar. There will be days you only have a few minutes, and other days you can spend more time. The important thing is to study knowing the Holy Spirit will guide, teach, and bring light to the word. It's not a chore. It's a time to meet with your Savior, Lord, and Friend. Grab a coffee or tea, get comfy, and expect Him to be there. Over time, this will bring so much light and purpose to your life.

Not only do we hear what God has to say when we read His word, but when we seek Him, we are sure to find Him. Finding Him is the best chance we have to heal.

II. Rich Prayer Life: Pray Always.

Prayer is something we can do anywhere and at any time. Make this a daily habit. For me, my routine started the first morning I woke up in my new home, which I had purchased after my divorce. I started by thanking God for sparing my life and for opening a way for me to exit the abuse when I hadn't seen a way out. I thanked Him for my beautiful house and for my lovable rescue cat.

Over time, this routine of praise evolved into a practice of prayer, a shield of protection that I cast over myself, my home, my family, and my new friends. It's a testament to the transformative power of prayer, a power that I believe is accessible to all who seek it.

> "Rejoice always, pray continually, give thanks in all circumstances; for this is God's will for you in Christ Jesus." (1 Thess 5:16-18)

Even though the following is regarding the Jewish people and their enemies, I do think we can extrapolate that it can refer to us today.

> "This is what the Lord says: 'When seventy years are completed for Babylon, I will come to you and fulfill my good promise to bring you back to this place. For I know the plans I have for you" declares the Lord, 'plans to prosper you and not to harm you, plans to give you hope and a future. Then you will call on me

and come and pray to me, and I will listen to you. You will seek me and find me when you seek me with all your heart. I will be found by you,' declares the Lord, ' and will bring you back from captivity." (Isa 29: 10-14)

When our hearts are surrendered to the Lord, He actively fights for us. This is a profound truth that I find incredibly reassuring: He *fights* for me. He fights for *me*. It doesn't matter where we place the emphasis in that phrase. God is not a passive observer in our lives. He is actively pursuing us, always ready to defend and protect us.

Why are we so often passive and even complacent? Or, worse yet, why do we actively run from him? Indeed, the enemy loves passivity because when we refuse to do our part and actively pursue God, the world comes between us and our Lord. The way to combat that is through prayer—unceasing prayer.

You may find your prayer time in the car while driving to work or having coffee in the quiet hours before your busy day starts. Once you have those times established, start praying throughout your day. Challenge yourself to always pray when something good or worrisome pops into your head. When the boss snips at you, pray that God will give you grace in handling the situation instead of worrying about what it did or didn't mean. Pray that your boss will be able to resolve his or her feelings and that there will be harmony in your job. Did you receive great news? Lift your voice in thanking God before you tell your mom or best friend. Make prayer a habit of being your mindset default.

If you're not sure how to start, I suggest praying for your closest friends and family. A great way to begin is simply asking God to provide them with the things they need. God already knows what they need so you don't even need to be specific in the beginning. As you strengthen your prayer muscles, you can ask the

Holy Spirit to guide you in your prayers so you can get in agreement with His will.

Here's an example of what I might pray. Your prayer can be simpler, shorter, and altogether different. This is just an illustration of how I start by acknowledging who God is and placing myself in the posture of thanksgiving.

"Heavenly Father, you are omnipotent, omniscient, and omnipresent. You are an awesome God, worthy of all my worship and praise and I thank you for all the blessings you've given me and especially for placing my dear friend Anna in my life. By the power of the Holy Spirit, give her the courage she needs today. Be present with her so that she feels that peace that surpasses all understanding. Guide her heart and her mind as she makes that difficult decision. Direct my conversation so that I can encourage her in a way that supports her and honors you. In the name of our Lord, Jesus Christ, Amen."

If you've never allocated a set time for focused prayer, now's a great time to start. Dedicated time helps me pray for all those who need it and I've found it immensely helpful to have a prayer journal. I love going back weeks and months later and seeing how many prayers have been answered! If you keep one long enough, you'll see how seemingly unanswered or "no's" were actually blessings. It's always fun to see how things have worked out in a way you could never have anticipated.

Prayer is powerful and will deepen your relationship with Jesus.

Rabid Prayer.

Audacious Prayer.

Continuous Prayer.

I've been told, "I'll pray for you on Sunday." Or "I already prayed about that." Or, flippantly, "I pray for things once and then drop it." I'm always surprised. Saving prayer for a certain day of the week isn't biblical. Praying for something once and being done? Situations evolve, which should mean our associated prayers should also evolve. He wants us to pray for others!

> "Therefore confess your sins to each other and pray for each other so that you may be healed. The prayer of a righteous person is powerful and effective." (James 5:16)

The closer we are to the person and the more we know about a situation, the more we can pray boldly and specifically. Sometimes, we are given discernment into a situation even the one asking for prayer cannot see. We need to bring that issue to God and ask him to open the eyes of their heart.

Scripture tells us to pray without ceasing, which means it should never end.

> "Rejoice always, [17] pray without ceasing, [18] give thanks in all circumstances; for this is the will of God in Christ Jesus for you." (1 Thess 5:16-18)

I learned how to pray from my mom. I pray in the morning, during work, and everywhere—in all I am doing. If I can't figure out a work problem, I pray. If my printer isn't working, I pray for troubleshooting knowledge. If I can't find something, I pray to recall where it is or for it to appear. I always find it.

Always.

You see, prayer for me is not a last resort; it's my first step. My entire life, I have kept an internal dialogue going with God. I ask Him questions. I talk through things with Him.

When someone asks for prayer, I pray. I lift that person up in prayer because I know God hears me.

After I remarried, my husband and I went through some tough financial times and our dryer stopped working. We couldn't afford a repairman, much less a new dryer. I laid hands on that dryer, and do you know, it remained working until we sold that house years later.

I pray for everything.

Everything.

A rich, unending prayer life keeps you plugged into the source of all life. Just as you focus on your friend when you meet for coffee, spending time in prayer with Jesus keeps you focused on him, no matter how your day goes.

The best thing is that you can do it while waiting in line, for a meeting to start, or when you can't sleep at night.

III. Finding Community: Seek Fellowship.

We grow exponentially by reading God's word, but we also grow when we are in fellowship with other believers. You can have your book reading club, but if you want to heal, if you want to see God transform your life, then you need to surround yourself with those who are plugged into God. They will not give you the world's response to your situation, but rather help you seek Jesus and understand what He has to say about it.

> "Walk with the wise and become wise, for a companion of fools suffers harm. Trouble pursues the sinner, but the righteous are rewarded with good things." (Proverbs 13:20-21)

Who you surround yourself matters. This is even more true for those of us who need to heal. We need Christian sisters (and brothers) to counsel us, to encourage us, and to pray for us. This takes a bit of bravery because you will have to open up. You are going to have to admit some things. You will need to allow people into your emotional life. It might feel like the last thing you want to do. Let me assure you that is just a lie from the enemy. When we open ourselves up and bring things that were previously hidden out into the light, healing can begin. Darkness will be replaced with the light of truth. Fear will subside with the love of new friends.

I recommend you join a Bible Study, so you get into a routine of meeting and studying God's word with other believers. Join a women's group. Women need other women. We need a trusted place where we can be honest about our struggles. This can be a place where the enemy will attack, so I'm warning you now that you will not 'fit' in just any group. You may have to try a few different types until you find one that clicks for you. There's nothing wrong with opting out of a group. It's nothing to feel bad about. Not every group is for everyone, and that's OK.

Find a group that meets your current needs. As you grow, you may need to move to a different group, and that's normal. The only caveat I want to add is don't just stop attending if you're feeling discomfort. Sometimes, when we're faced with our own brokenness we bristle and like to blame the group for what we see in the mirror.

Remember, healing can only happen when we recognize and appropriately dress a wound. It's the same with emotional healing. We must recognize our own brokenness that led us into the abusive relationship. Then we should be willing to face our unhealthy thinking and sinful habits we haven't addressed. One way to test this is to pay attention to where the discomfort is coming from. Be honest. Is it because we don't like what we hear, causing something inside us to feel unsettled? Or is someone in the group making you feel ashamed by how they speak to you? Shame is when someone makes you feel "less than" by acting superior.

People and Satan condemn and shame. God reveals and convicts. The Holy Spirit calls us to become more and more, not less than. No one shaming us is speaking for God.

It can be confusing, especially when we've lived our entire lives under another person's emotional control and manipulation. I found that when I first faced my own sinfulness, I felt shame, not because that is who God is but because that's what I equated to my weaknesses being exposed. The hot burning sensation that coursed through my veins that I'd become so accustomed to from being raged at also plagued me in the first few years of healing from the trauma. I had to learn that it wasn't God making me feel shame. This is why it is so critical to be reading scripture, so we read the word of God and learn the difference.

> "Therefore there is no condemnation now for those who are in Christ Jesus because through Christ Jesus the law of the Spirit who gives life has set you free from the law of sin and death." (Rom 8:1-2)

It is imperative to be in communion with other believers so that we can talk about these things openly and honestly, without judgment.

IV. Serving: Focus on Other People

Serving others is the best way to put our own problems in perspective. When we focus on helping others, we become acutely aware of other people's needs, and it minimizes our own needs. It's also a great way to recognize and give thanks for what we have and what is going right in our lives.

Serving in church connects us with our fellow believers and the body of Christ. Even in our hurting and brokenness, God can use us to bring hope and encouragement to someone else.

I have found that when I felt as if I had nothing to give, those were the times when God spoke through me to someone. It's not me saying what I think God wants me to say; rather, when I am completely empty, that is when I know it's God working.

Perhaps you'll want to find ways to share your story and help others who share a similar experience. Maybe you're just in a spot where you need to show up, roll up your sleeves, and quietly work painting, weeding, planting, and serving food. These are tasks that help others out and allow you to momentarily get outside of yourself for a while.

When we witness God using us to bless another person, we are assured that He is with us and working, even if we don't see movement in a particular area of our lives.

This is why I believe it is crucial that we crawl outside of ourselves to serve others—it is a double blessing! If we stay holed up at home or hide behind computer screens, we limit the avenues God has to use in others' lives.

There is a lie perpetuated by our culture, dare I even say the church culture, that we must be "whole" or "healed" before we can serve or help others. In this area, God and his miracles show up and throw a wrench in that theory. I have witnessed women in the depths of their own suffering be able to offer words of encouragement to lift other women up, to offer hope, and to extend compassion to others walking a similar journey.

God works when we are serving others.

It is through obedience in serving that I found another level of healing.

V. Forgiving: You and Everyone Else

You may have a hard time forgiving the one who abused you. Maybe you have said, "I can't forgive him," but the reality isn't that you can't, it's that you won't. I've found that forgiveness isn't allowing the abuser to continue to perpetuate violence on you, nor is forgiveness equal to forgetting what happened.

Forgiveness is letting go of all the hate in your heart for that person so you can live freely. Forgiveness is recognizing that they are broken and living in a broken world just as we are. Jesus tells us forgiveness isn't an option. We must because He forgave us.

"You were once at odds with God." *(Col 1:21 – 22)*

It's a decision, not a feeling. I contend you won't feel forgiveness until you've extended it. Decide to forgive. Verbalize it and announce it out loud. Make a firm statement of forgiving the other person. If you don't feel that you have it in you to forgive, then that is the very thing you should pray for – that you would be able to forgive.

We forgive others because God instructs us to do so. He will take care of the rest. When we're finally in heaven married to Christ, serving, and reigning with Him, our relationships with each other will also be perfect – devoid of sin. Thinking about that makes forgiving easier because I know all this earthly stuff will be behind us one day. Any relationships taken out by sin in this life will be perfect in the next life. The hopeful expectation is that one day, we will live in perfect unity. Now that's something to look forward to!

While you're at it, be sure you forgive yourself too.

One of the best ways to let go of the past is to create a new present reality. That means changing things up and doing things differently. Hate the town you live in but love your job? Relocate within commuting distance. Love your town but share the church with your ex? Find a new church. Love your town but feel isolated? Join clubs or organizations that get you out of your house and involved in your community.

There is always another path. I've learned that even when we can't see a path, God will create one for us. He will make a way where we see no way.

As I was putting the finishing touches on this book, I struggled with how to finish it. I wondered how I would publish it or if it would ever make a difference to anyone. All I could see were the obstacles, and I kept thinking about everything that could go wrong with publishing something so deeply personal. I prayed for guidance for weeks as I struggled with thoughts of abandoning this project altogether.

After about two weeks of internal debate, I had a vivid dream. In this dream, I saw two ways to move forward in publishing. Then, God pulled me up into the heavens so I could see his view, and there were no less than 20 winding paths, all leading the same way. In the dream, I realized that my human mind could never comprehend all those possibilities because I was too limited in thinking. But our omnipotent God has ways to make things work that we cannot even fathom. I woke up determined to continue on – writing in faith.

Don't worry about how He's going to work. Your job is to keep getting up each day, drawing close to him, and staying proactive and productive. God will create the opportunities and pathways.

VI. Christian Counseling: Practical Healing

We often can't heal by ourselves. Isolation and holding it all in for years has led us to our present circumstances, so don't pretend to be something you aren't. If you were strong enough to stand up to your abuser, you wouldn't be where you are today. Be honest with yourself and open enough to realize that there are mental health professionals who can help you on your journey. They can provide you with tools that will help you figure out what went wrong and help you move forward.

A good counselor will not keep you as a patient for years on end; instead, she will equip you to reshape your way of thinking, help you reframe, and, most importantly, avoid repeating past mistakes.

If you are a Christian, find a female Christian counselor. It was beneficial to have someone encouraging and holding me accountable according to a Godly standard.

Even if you got out before it led to years of abuse, I want to encourage you to engage in Christian counseling to help you recalibrate because even if your abuse was short-lived, there are very likely some things you need to work through. Something made you attracted to him or him to you. Something kept you in it. That something needs to be healed.

I would not have been able to move forward without the help of my counselor, Gail. I am eternally grateful to her, for she was the one who was able to identify things that had become normal but that were very much abnormal and unhealthy. She helped me uncover patterns of beliefs and behaviors that had led me into this marriage. I would not be where I am today without her guidance.

"And this is my prayer: that your love may abound more and more in knowledge and depth of insight, so that you may be able to discern what is best and may be pure and blameless for the day of Christ, filled with the fruit of righteousness that comes through Jesus Christ—to the glory and praise of God." (Phil 1:9-11)

CHAPTER 17
PSYCHOLOGICAL VIOLENCE

If you are a pastor or leader in a position to counsel or advise those who are in abusive marriages, please consider the points in this Chapter. These things can be equally helpful if you are a friend or family member.

Ever since breaking free of the abuse, I have been compelled to help other women. As I got involved at my church with their program for those who were hurting, it became clear that what I experienced was not uncommon. This drives me to call attention to this issue of abuse within Christian marriages.

When I first encountered the term "psychological violence," I stopped. Something deep inside me stirred. It was just like that feeling when you're in a crowd and see that friend you're meeting. First, you subconsciously recognize their face, and then your heart and face catch up as you smile and wave, feeling a little lighter at having spotted them. When I read those words, I noticed that something previously unsettled had been recognized deep within me.

Validated.

A question I didn't even know I was asking had been answered. A lifetime of fractured feelings suddenly made sense.

"Words matter," our culture says. This is perhaps the one thing we, as Christians, can agree on with the secular world.

> "The tongue has the power of life and death, and
> those who love it will eat its fruit." (Proverbs 18:21)

If you've ever learned a second language, no doubt you've learned the hard way that words have multiple meanings in every language, which our modern culture overlooks. One of the reasons I adore reading is because books have expanded my vocabulary in a productive way unrivaled by any other hobby or form of entertainment. I've always been intrigued by the lesser-known meanings of words, so when I discovered "violence" didn't just mean a physical manifestation of negative emotions, I was fascinated. That may be the most popular use in our culture, but it certainly is not the only meaning.

When I read "psychological violence," so many things started to make sense to me. I understood why I had started experiencing panic attacks and why my entire body would feel cold and tingly when experiencing the verbal outbursts, the harsh words, the accusations, the lies, the sneers, the rants, the name-calling, and the rages. Those violent assaults may not have manifested in physical blows, but they certainly affected me in a very deep psychological way and manifested physiologically as well.

If you've been subject to chronic, nonsensical, screaming rage or incessant biting criticism of one who speaks to you with utter disgust and heaps shame on you and controls you, then you understand that those hate-filled outbursts are, indeed, violent.

It is devastating.

It is lasting.

When not stopped, it gets passed down as a generational behavior. The cycle continues from mother to daughter to granddaughter, from husband to wife to child, to the next generation, again and again.

Although it is being talked about more now than ever, emotional abuse is downplayed because physical abuse has taken center stage as the worst of all domestic crimes, short of murder.

During my life, I've watched people's faces seem to change when they think someone has been a victim of physical abuse and learn it was "just" emotional abuse. It is as if the word "abuse" carries no weight at all, and the preceding adverb is what dictates the listener's level of empathy.

To get us all on the same page, let's look at the dictionary definition of the word abuse, which is:

1. a corrupt practice or custom
2. improper or excessive use or treatment
3. language that condemns or vilifies usually unjustly, intemperately, and angrily
4. physical maltreatment

This is why I must point out the injustice done to all of us who have suffered from chronic emotional abuse, a.k.a. psychological violence, and have been dismissed or otherwise ignored when it comes to seeking help. We will talk about all sorts of other abuses that are completely unacceptable and we would never treat the subject with the cavalier attitude with which we talk about emotional abuse.

I'd like to see us all stop treating the word "abuse" as if that word alone isn't bad enough. We don't need to qualify it, just like we don't need to say 'date-raped' versus 'stranger-raped.' Let's stop qualifying the word abuse.

Physical abuse is wrong.

Emotional abuse is wrong.

Both lead to long-lasting psychological effects.

When you are in proximity to counsel or lend an ear, please keep the following seven points in mind:

I. Be honest with yourself.

First, be honest about your relationship with this person. Understand how close you are or aren't. Have they approached you for help, or do you recognize the dysfunction and desire to help?

Unsolicited advice rarely goes over well in any scenario, and it's especially unwelcome when we expose something the other person would rather keep hidden. When those of us in an abusive situation are still in denial, any type of offense from the outside can cause us to run in the abuser's defense and delay the exodus. Sick, I know, but that was my reality, and I'm sure I'm not unique. Avoid the temptation to "fix" them or their relationship.

Second, be honest about your feelings toward this person. Do you have a history that makes you less or overly sympathetic to them? Leaders: did this person oppose your idea in a committee meeting? Has this person's spouse been a large contributor financially to your church? If this is your sister-in-law, are you struggling to believe your brother could really be abusive? Good or bad experiences with the individual or family members can significantly impact our level of empathy. You have a solemn responsibility to honestly evaluate whether you can counsel this person unbiasedly and in a Godly manner. If you cannot, recuse yourself and refer them to a Christian counselor or someone who can be objective.

The same applies if you are a friend or family member. What you say can be as impactful as what comes from a church leader. Check your motives. It doesn't matter if you want them to stay or leave the relationship. This is not about what you want or think. Don't get trapped in what you want the outcome to be. Recognize your biases, and if you cannot be objective, help direct the person to someone who can.

Perhaps you're a mom with several little kids and don't have the time to listen and counsel a friend through hours of conversation. Do what you can, but don't compromise your own boundaries. We'll never meet everyone's needs all the time, so don't feel bad about it. Be honest if you are not the right person. Admit it to yourself – and to them.

If you're a pastor or lay leader, don't take on counseling because you're "supposed" to have all the answers. If you come across someone who needs mental health help, reach out to your network for a trusted Christian counselor that you can refer her to. You can provide guidance in spiritual development as she seeks counseling. If you have no training or experience with psychological violence, don't pretend you do. Don't presume you'll have the answers simply because you're a pastor. It's OK not to have all the answers or even any answers for that matter. Provide the help you can with humility, so you actively recruit the right type of help for the person in need. There's a reason why Christian counseling is a vocation – there's a need for it.

II. Understand Your Role.

The primary role of a pastor is not to keep a church member from getting a divorce; rather, Jesus calls you to shepherd your flock. That means encouragement. Shepherding is taken seriously by God. If this is you, read the entire chapter of Ezekial 34. Let's just look at the first few verses.

> "The word of the LORD came to me: "Son of man, prophesy against the shepherds of Israel; prophesy and say to them: 'This is what the Sovereign LORD says: Woe to you shepherds of Israel who only take care of yourselves! Should not shepherds take care of the flock? You eat the curds, clothe yourselves with the wool and slaughter the choice animals, but you do not take care of the flock. You have not strengthened the weak or healed the sick or bound up the injured. You have not brought back the strays or searched for the lost. You have ruled them harshly and brutally. ⁵ So they were scattered because there was no shepherd, and when they were scattered they became food for all the wild animals. My sheep wandered over all the mountains and on every high hill. They were scattered over the whole earth, and no one searched or looked for them. "'Therefore, you shepherds, hear the word of the LORD: As surely as I live, declares the Sovereign LORD, because my flock lacks a shepherd and so has been plundered and has become food for all the wild animals, and because my shepherds did not search for my flock but cared for themselves rather than for my flock, therefore, you shepherds, hear the word of the LORD: This is what the Sovereign LORD says: I am against the shepherds and will hold them accountable for my flock. I will remove them from tending the flock so that the shepherds can no longer feed themselves. I will rescue my flock from their mouths, and it will no longer be food for them." (Ezekiel 34:1-10)

Ezekial is full of warnings to shepherds. Shepherds will be held accountable. Matthew Henry's commentary on this chapter, *"Now in this chapter the shepherds of Israel, their rulers both in church and state, are called to an account, as having been very much accessory to the sin and ruin of Israel, by their neglecting to do the duty of their place. A high charge exhibited against them for their negligence, their unskillfulness, and unfaithfulness in the management of public affairs."*

It is incumbent on you to handle things in a Godly manner. Being unskilled was not an excuse but was viewed as negligence. You don't have to have first-hand experience of neglect or abuse in order to minister to someone. However, you do need to approach it from a shepherding perspective, which means to tend to, guard, and guide.

One way to minister to a hurting person is simply to listen. When those of us who have been abused for years finally start talking, there is emotional volatility that may make little sense to the listener. This is part of our process. Ask clarifying questions if you don't understand something. This will help you piece things together.

Encourage her in her spiritual walk. If you encourage daily scripture reading and getting involved in the church community, she will start to receive healing simply by drawing nearer to Jesus. Remember, we don't need you to have answers. Initially, we need to be heard. Shepherd, guide, and encourage us.

In the early stages of sharing, we still want to protect our spouse. We are so traumatized that we are not yet ready to reveal everything. Afraid of judgment, we won't share every last detail, and therefore, I beg you not to judge but to listen. Be Jesus in the flesh for us. Jesus doesn't condemn. He lovingly holds us and points us to what is better, which pierces our hearts and compels us to be better. To live better. Condemnation causes us to run and hide in shame. When someone opens up to you, please do not cause them to feel any more shame than they already do. Rather, be like Jesus, who can hear the worst and still love.

If you are a friend or family member, you may not be the right person to give counseling advice, but you can listen. Maybe it's your sister, who you are close to and never have liked your brother-in-law. There can be a thing as being "too close" to a situation. Instead of offering godly counsel, you can easily get caught up in the drama and gossip about the abuser, which doesn't resolve anything. Be clear about what your role is. A simple, "I don't have any experience with this, but I can listen if you want to share" can go a long way in allowing one to start opening up.

If you're unable to encourage – spiritual or otherwise, simply commiserating isn't productive, and it's not going to help her through or out of anything. You, too, can be the one to nudge her to professional Christian counseling.

III. Pray & Activate the Holy Spirit

Pray before encounters with the person. Pray that God will open pathways of communication and open their minds. Pray for the Holy Spirit to activate in you to direct your words. Pray for the Holy Spirit to activate in the life of the person coming to speak with you.

Prayerfully seek what God wants to say to her. I find that when we do this, we go from a tone of telling someone how they should act, feel, or live to a tone of encouragement. Instead of hearing how stupid she is or how awful her abuser is, speak of what God wants for her as a believer.

I have found myself in the position to counsel women who were abusive spouses. That was not an easy situation for a person with my past. Through prayer, I met the need that God placed before me. I didn't have to lie and tell her it was OK. I didn't have to feel bitter that I was offering encouragement to the one causing the pain; all I did was pray that the Holy Spirit show me what to say, and He did. The beautiful part is that we'll never go wrong when we seek His advice. When we have no idea what to say, we can expect the Holy Spirit to show up and give us the words that are needed. We don't have to force anything because when we invite the Holy Spirit into the conversation, He answers.

IV. Speak Truth and Speak Up

Keep speaking the truth. If you witness something or hear something abusive, speak up! It may be the first time they've heard it. The first time I heard, "Leah, that's emotionally abusive," I had to sit with that for a long time as I processed what that meant. I didn't dismiss it. It was shining light into the darkness. It was picking the end of a string so I could unwind and unravel years of conditioning.

As a friend or family member, you may have opportunities to speak up when you witness wrong behavior. Men, especially if you are a father or brother, your authority is needed. Joe was mean and abusive in public or in front of family members many times. No one said anything, which was disheartening. Not once did anyone come to my defense. Not only did the lack of chastisement embolden Joe, but it also further enforced the distorted view I had of myself and our relationship. Had someone just once said during one of those instances, "That's not very nice, Joe." Or "That's abusive language, Joe." Had any of the women in my life pulled me aside and said something like, "When he spoke to you, that wasn't very loving. I hope you know he shouldn't speak to you that way." Anything, anything, would have helped me know others saw it too. I desperately needed outside validation for what I felt was the truth, but no one ever came to my defense, so I didn't speak of it for fear of being labeled as difficult or ungodly.

Speaking the truth brings things to light. We need more light in our world. We need more truth spoken. When you hear language in children playing together, if you see it in a couple dating, if you see it happening to your son or daughter, do not ignore it. I felt at times as if I had been sold off into slavery because no one cared about me enough to speak up. I felt abandoned, and the abuse Joe heaped out led me to believe I deserved every bit of it.

V. Educate Yourself on Trauma.

This is a pervasive cultural problem that isn't improving. If you're a pastor, don't ignore it. You can provide help and healing to those who have experienced or are experiencing trauma.

If you're a friend or family member of someone living in abuse, please remember they are hurting. Trauma is psychologically damaging. We can obstruct a person's avenue of healing by imparting judgment on their circumstances. Unless you live behind closed doors with someone, you'll never know who they are. Accept that you don't know and never will know every last ugly detail. Also, accept that you don't have to agree with someone or their choices to offer them hope.

I believe God is raising awareness nationwide about this issue, both in our secular culture and within the church. If your heart is being stirred, ask God how He would direct you and your ministry in this area. Ministering is a privilege. Perhaps you are being called to meet this need in your church and your community.

VI. Teach About Standards.

God has a standard. Christians are to be set apart. God even has boundaries! We are instructed to enforce boundaries on what we view and think about. Everything about boundaries is biblical. I would like the church to talk about how to treat people beyond the catchphrase of "Kindness." I didn't know I could stand up to those who used snarky jabs and belittling comments. I knew it stung, but the message that was reinforced throughout my childhood was that I should be concerned about everyone else's feelings at my own expense. I didn't hear anything different at church.

Culture provides us with such an abomination of communication that we no longer know what constitutes respectful speech. I'd love to hear our pastors talk about an appropriate way to speak to one another and what healthy conversation is like. I would rejoice if I heard a sermon about identifying and standing up against manipulation, deceit, passive aggressiveness, and any form of unhealthy communication.

VII. Equip Your Church.

As our sin-sick culture deteriorates, the need is only going to increase. Pray for this ministry opportunity.

A first step would be to encourage and facilitate women's groups so women have a community and a venue for cultivating meaningful, God-honoring friendships.

Another answer could mean identifying and equipping leaders who can walk alongside women in crisis and putting a plan in place so that your church is prepared to meet that need when a hurting woman comes to you seeking help.

It could also look like partnering with a Christian counseling center so you can point women to help.

AFTERWORD

I am delighted to have read Leah's book. The book she birthed from the pain of her abusive marriage. God turned her turmoil into triumph - her pain into victory. "And we know that in all things God works for the good of those who love Him, who have been called according to his purpose." (Rom 8:28)

Leah has used what she has painfully learned in walking through the extensive healing process, and God is using her experience to help other women who find themselves somewhere in her story. And with God's help, you, too, will find victory.

Inexperienced women don't know what red flags are. I have a meme saved on my phone. "Therapist:

You saw the red flags, though, right? Me: I thought it was a carnival." You don't know that what you see is a red flag because you have never experienced a red flag before. For example, if you grew up in a home where your father abused your mother, you think it's "normal" and don't question what you are now experiencing in your marriage. "Red Flags" are like icebergs; only 5-15% of the red flag is visible, and the other 85-95% is below the surface. That little red flag you see looks kind of cute, but it's not cute: THAT is just the tip of the iceberg.

As Leah and I talked about her manuscript, I asked her if Joe had ever been physically abusive to her, and she said that he had kicked her a few times in public on an airport shuttle, but he hadn't ever hit her. She was just her husband's verbal punching bag.

It still amazes me when I work with my female clients who are in abusive relationships that they only think being hit is abuse or domestic violence. In recent years, intimidation is now considered domestic violence. Ladies, if you are trying to call someone for help and your phone is ripped out of your hand and thrown across the room, that is domestic violence. If you are trying to leave the house and your way out is being blocked, that is domestic violence.

As Leah said, and many women would say, "I should have known." No. There are things we know that we know. I know that I'm a pretty good therapist. There are things we know that we don't know. I know that I do not know how to play the piano or golf. Then, there are things that we don't even know we don't know because we have never experienced those things and we don't recognize them. You cannot blame yourself for not recognizing these lies and deception if you've never experienced them.

Deceptive men [and women] have their behavior down pat. Don't think you are the first person your husband has ever done this to. He did it to his former girlfriends or former wife. Men [and women] who deceive have perfected their skills of deception. How would an "ordinary" person recognize something they've never seen or experienced? They don't know. For the most part, an abuser does not abuse you before "sealing the deal." I had a client whose husband turned into someone she didn't recognize during the reception. It was too late. Who was this guy? And yet, she stayed married to him for five years.

If you let the first lie [or deception] go, you will excuse the 2nd, 3rd, 4th, 5th, and 10th lie!!

Sometimes, you still don't know what it is until your girlfriend or a therapist who has been through something like what you are going through identifies the red flag. Even though a girlfriend may say the same thing a therapist would say, you, like Leah, defend and excuse him. So those same words coming from a therapist pack a mightier punch and are much more believable than if a girlfriend says it.

The saying, "You can't see the forest for the trees" is a perfect example of what you are experiencing. You're right smack dab in the middle of the forest, but all you see are the trees immediately surrounding you and you don't recognize the abuse. You're too emotionally close and you don't see the big picture. Your girlfriend, sister, or your therapist are 100 yards away and can see the entire forest – the big picture. They are not emotionally attached to your boyfriend or husband and can see things you don't see.

A lot of churches or pastors tiptoe around marital abuse. And yes, they say, "Pray about it" or "get into a couples bible study together." Or they may remind you that on your wedding day, the pastor said, "What God has joined together, let no man [or lawyer] put asunder." Or "God hates divorce!!!" So, stay married no matter what. God may hate divorce, but God does not want His daughters to be abused in any way, shape, or form.

In the mid-90s, I worked in a Christian organization, Wheaton College in Wheaton, IL, and Moody Bible Institute. I had to fill in for the receptionist while she took her lunch break, and I heard a woman on the Christian radio station playing in the lobby say, "Women, if you're being abused in your marriage, just take it for Jesus." I was appalled by what I heard, and I thought, "Lady, you're going to get someone killed."

God gives women "gut instinct," and time after time, I have heard women say, "If I had only listened to my gut . . ."

Ladies, listen to your gut!!!

Gail L. Logemann, LMFT

RESOURCES

The following is a list of books and resources I found immensely important in my path to healing. Not all are Christian authors, but each was critical in restoring my emotional and mental health. I have found this an ongoing process as my thought patterns and behaviors were formed in childhood. I must stay vigilant, constantly monitoring my relationships with others and paying attention to my reactions and responses to living with healthy boundaries in all areas of my life.

Boundaries: When to say yes, when to say no to take control of your life by Dr. John Townsend and Dr. Henry Cloud is a foundational book for any healthy relationship and a bookshelf staple for those who grew up without boundaries. I've read it five times and learned more each time.

The Emotionally Healthy Woman by Geri & Peter Scazzero. Watch the accompanying videos to this book to hear them share their powerful story. This would likely resonate with you if you grew up in the church.

The Men Who Hate Women and the Women Who Love Them by Dr Susan Howard & Joann Torres. If you are, or were, in a narcissistic relationship, you need to read this one.

Experiencing God: Knowing and Doing the Will of God by Henry & Richard Blackaby and Claude V. King provides fantastic instruction on how to walk more closely with God.

Walking in Victory: Why God's love can change your life like legalism never could by Dennis McCallum. If you have accepted

Jesus as your Savior but have not yet understood that you have already been forgiven, this book is a must! Once you enter this covenant, his substitution or atoning sacrifice has already been made, and his blood covers your sin. Once you repent and receive him as your personal savior and understand all that entails, you will be able to forgive yourself and live under the covering of his grace.

Deliverance and Spiritual Warfare Manual by John Eckhardt. This book is fire! I wish more Christians would learn that we have the power to overcome spiritual strongholds.

Captivating: Unveiling the Mystery of the Woman's Soul by John & Stasi Eldredge and *Wild at Heart: Discovering the Secret to a Man's Soul* by John Eldredge. Both explore God's plan for his magnificent creation and how sin destroys that.

Jesus in Me: Experiencing the Holy Spirit as a Constant Companion by Ann Graham Lotz. Written by Billy Graham's daughter, it was the first book I ever read specifically on the Holy Spirit.

Graham Cooke: Brilliant Perspectives Podcast. Graham challenges us to focus on our friendship with Jesus.

The Four Agreements by Don Miguel Ruiz. If you want to avoid the new-age precepts, just skip right to the chapter on the agreements. This book helped me recalibrate after years of living with lies and half-truths.

Dr. Ramani Durvasula: YouTube channel & podcast. A clinical psychologist and retired professor of psychology, Dr. Ramani is an expert in narcissistic personality disorder.

ACKNOWLEDGMENTS

Thank you to my husband, Sean, for giving me space when I needed to write. On those days, I scoured old journals and endured depressive moods. Sean was patient and understanding, knowing I had to travel back into the past to get this all out. That catharsis was necessary to write honestly.

Thank you to all who contributed in a significant way to bringing this book to completion:

My dear friend Marjorie Stradinger, for pouring her love and passion into this by offering careful review and feedback. Her editorial expertise, Scriptural knowledge, and love for Jesus were invaluable. She was the crucial woman in my life during my exodus from that abusive relationship, so it was apropos to be the one who helped me get this across the finish line.

Thank you, Ann Kafer, for thoughtfully editing and offering a ministry perspective and a sounding board for areas that required more work. Her support helped me over a writing plateau.

Erich Hofmeister, for providing insight and recommendations from a pastoral and counseling point of view in the book's early stages and for writing a beautiful Foreword.

Gail Logemann, for guiding me to the path of healing all those years ago as my Christian counselor. She helped me learn a healthy way of thinking and I was honored she was willing to lend her name and credentials for the Afterword.

Pastor Cameron Graper, thank you for discussing the concepts of this book from a ministry perspective. The Holy Spirit affirmed this project through you.

Finally, to those who read the early drafts, and despite the crude form of the early manuscript, still offered encouragement and critical feedback: Cyndi Bowers, Melissa Hayden, Tess Kossow, Jackie Schroeder, and James Serpento.

"Every ending will meet its own end, for every ending is destined to be swallowed up by a beginning."

Craig D. Lounsbrough

ABOUT THE AUTHOR

Leah Hoppes is a versatile author who crafts engaging narratives that captivate readers. Her commitment to authenticity infuses her work with depth and honesty that is both refreshing and engaging. Leah's passion for helping women mature in their Christian faith is evident in her latest work, making her a compelling voice in Christian Nonfiction.

www.leahhoppes.com

www.ingramcontent.com/pod-product-compliance
Lightning Source LLC
LaVergne TN
LVHW041221080426
835508LV00011B/1022